On Undefended Flesh
The memoir of an obedient girl

Shana Shine

This is a work of non-fiction. However, names and other identifying features have been changed to protect identities. The author has warranted to the publishers that, except in such minor respects not affecting the substantial accuracy of the work, the contents of this book are true.

Flicking Lizard Ltd.
176c Hartfield Road,
Wimbledon, London SW19 3TQ

The website address is www.flickinglizard.co.uk

First published in 2009

© Shana Shine 2009

Shana Shine asserts the moral right to be identified as the author of this work

Cover design © Rob Bocci
boc.rob@googlemail.com

A catalogue record of this book is available from the British Library

ISBN 978-0-9559531-1-8

All rights reserved. No part of this publication may be reproduced, stored in a retrieval system, or transmitted, in any form or by any means, electronic, mechanical, photocopying, recording or otherwise, without the prior written permission of the publishers.

Printed and bound in Great Britain by CPI Cox & Wyman, Reading, RG1 8EX

Thanks to my publisher.

And thanks Nicky.

Contents

Cleaning and Hoovering	1
Job-Search Misery	12
Funny Business in Brighton	17
Going Professional	23
My Chelsea Master – Part 1	29
My Chelsea Master – Part 2	55
Falling in Love with my Daddy	67
New Clients On-Board	102
Daddy's Little Girl	118
Torn	147
Little Girl's Broken Heart	188
Mick's Bitch	222
Trick or Treat	248
Game Over, Daddy	268
Public Humiliation	279
New Beginnings?	293

Prologue:

Cleaning and Hoovering

I move towards his feet, getting closer and closer. It's pitch black outside with only a dim, eerie light entering the room. The door is closed and I feel absolutely vulnerable.

'Lick my shoes clean.'

I turn my head up towards him, hoping what I had just heard was somehow not real. However, one glance into those piercing blue eyes, there is no more doubt.

I run my tongue over the smooth leather.

'Lick the sole, too.'

I try and avoid it, but he's staring down vigilantly, making sure I obey. As I'm licking his sole I hear the shocking sound of him unzipping his trousers ... and then rubbing his penis. I do not look up, I do not want to see it, so I just concentrate on his shoes.

'Fucking bitch! You are a useless little slut, aren't you?'

'Yes, I am.'

'Useless cunt! You should have been born dead. You are nothing but a filthy shit. Do you understand?'

'Yes, I do,' I respond from my position on the floor.

'You're just another eastern European whore. You are disgusting.'

'Yes, I am ... *disgusting*.'

As my tears fall I can hear him getting turned on, hear him breathing heavily.

'Crawl to the fireplace right now and lick it clean.'

It's opposite the sofa, so I crawl there on all fours and begin licking the stone all the way round; I can sense his penetrating stare on my thighs and bottom, which are visible when I lean down to get my tongue into the corners. I'm there cleaning for some time before he barks out his next commands.

'Go to the kitchen and get two big glasses from the cupboard. Fill them with water and then come back.'

I find the biggest glasses I can and then fill them up, all the while wondering what he is going to do with them. When I return he's still standing there masturbating, looking at me with disgust.

'Useless little slut. Drink the water in your right hand.'

Cleaning and Hoovering

I begin taking mouthfuls of the water.

'Quickly!' he orders.

He watches attentively as the water goes down, saturating my body.

'Now drink the other one.'

Only with considerable effort do I manage to force all the contents of the second glass down.

'You can carry on now crawling around the table.'

I begin crawling. Though I try and hold on, it is only a few minutes later that my small bladder begs me to stop.

'May I go to the toilet, please?' I ask, having no idea how he will respond.

He smiles sarcastically. I can see in his face this is exactly what he has been waiting for.

'Slut. You have two options, as I am generous: you do not go to the toilet … or you do. But if you go, you will be severely punished.'

'What?' I protest meekly.

'I won't repeat it, you ugly piece of shit!' he yells furiously.

But I don't have the luxury of choice; I rush to the nearby bathroom to relieve myself. Closing the door shut behind me, I search for a lock but find none.

Long after finishing, I remain seated on the toilet, crying, dreading the moment I will have to come out …

On Undefended Flesh

'Hello. I saw your ad on Gumtree. Do you still require a job?' His voice sounds posh and very strict.

'Yes, I do,' I reply, hopeful. Had I finally found someone who would help me out of this job-search misery?

'Good, as I have a vacancy for a cleaner who would join the team of maids already working in my apartment.'

'What kind of work is involved?'

'Basically providing cleanliness to a very high standard. Hoovering, dusting, washing, serving my meals to the table — that sort of thing.'

'That would be no problem, I can do all that. And where are you based?' I ask enthusiastically.

'I live in High Street Kensington.' He pauses; it sounds like he is searching for the best way to say something. 'But I have to point out that you need to be very **obedient**.'

'What do you mean?' I ask, worried that my English may not be good enough to understand the full meaning of the word.

'You must obey some strict rules. You have to be extremely precise, immaculate and punctual.'

'Well, I can work hard and take pride in whatever I do,' I say, not sure if this is what he means.

'Excellent! You'll also wear a uniform that I provide.'

'OK.' (I'm surprised to hear this, but perhaps he wants all the maids to look the same.)

'And you have to call me "Master" at all times.'

'Master ... ' I repeat the word anxiously.

'Yes. Do you understand?' he asks, his voice rather arrogant.

Cleaning and Hoovering

'I do,' I reply, beginning to feel unnerved.

'I'm holding interviews tonight. I will be paying for the interview as well.'

'Really?'

'Yes, twenty pounds. The applicants will be required to complete various small tasks on which I can test them. So will you be coming tonight?'

I hesitate. It all kind of sounds mysterious.

'Not to worry. There are several applicants, so if you don't think you are suitable, that's all right. But you have to let me know right now if you are coming, as this vacancy needs to be filled urgently.'

'Are you really going to pay for the interview? Even if you are not satisfied?'

'I certainly will,' he says adamantly.

I try and force my misgivings aside, telling myself that the English have their own peculiar way of doing things. Perhaps he is just another one of these eccentric Englishmen that I've always read about.

'What is your address?' I finally ask.

'_____ Road. 9pm.'

'Could we meet in a public place first?'

'All right,' he says. 'We can meet at High Street Kensington tube. But don't be late.'

'No, I won't.'

'You forgot something,' he says angrily.

There's a pause as I try and work out what it could possibly be.

'To address me properly,' he adds.
'Oh yes, Master. I do apologise, Master.'
'That's it!' He gives a loud and ironic laugh.

The bus arrives at the station. It's freezing outside, the cold only amplifying my fear. I take up a spot discreetly by a corner, and begin scrutinising men as they go by, wondering who could be my so-called master. Though I have no idea what he looks like, I'm expecting someone dominant and powerful.

And here he comes ... it must be him. He cannot see me, but he's turning his head in different directions, obviously looking for someone. I approach him. When I'm only a few feet away I begin to feel a strange sensation: an overpowering combination of fear, excitement, obedience and weakness. All my energy deserts me and my limbs start shivering with cold ... and I cannot understand why.

He turns and sees me. He looks frightening — a tall, solidly-built man with intense blue eyes, and the most gigantic ears I have ever seen. He's staring at me with an arrogant grin that makes me feel small and helpless; my mind is telling me to go home straight away.

'I came for the interview,' I mumble shyly.
'Good,' he says, with a strict voice that I recognise in an instant. *'Then let's go.'*
'I don't know. Maybe I shouldn't.'
'Why?'
'I'm afraid of you,' I tell him honestly.
He gives me a wicked smile that does nothing to appease

Cleaning and Hoovering

my fear.

'It would be a shame if you didn't come. You would make a good maid,' he encourages me.

Vacillating, I try and summon up courage. Though it's dangerous, isn't this exactly why I've come to London ... to get out of my comfort zone, take chances, do things I would never normally consider doing? Shouldn't I be opening myself up to the world of possibilities? Besides, in my position, any money, even twenty pounds, would be welcome.

'Well, just to let you know, my friends are at a café nearby. They know the address where we're going.'

'That's very sensible,' he says, unperturbed.

He starts walking and I follow. We soon arrive at his home — a fairly modest apartment. (Why on earth would he need a team of maids, I wonder?) He leads me into a room where lying on the bed are the maid uniforms in an assortment of sizes.

'Now choose the right size. Put on a white shirt, skirt, black tights and heels. Change quickly then come upstairs.'

When he leaves I select some items and change into them. I glance in the mirror and notice the outfit makes me look slutty. Having never worn high heels before, I clamber my way upstairs. Eventually I reach the living room, where I find him seated comfortably on a sofa.

'Come here.'

I move to the sofa awkwardly, hesitating on where exactly to stand.

'Stand in front of me.' His voice and eyes are exceptionally stern, making me feel as though I were now before the devil.

He inspects me thoroughly, checking me from head to toe.

'Turn around.'

'Turn to the right.'

'To the left.'

'To the right again.'

'To the left ...' *He carries on with these turning commands until I become dizzy.*

'Kneel down on the floor.'

'Crawl around the table ...' *And I do everything he asks of me. I'm surprised how obedient I am, crawling around on my hands and knees like a little dog around a table; but my intuition tells me that if I disobey this man things will only turn nasty ...*

'Get the fuck out, you bitch!' He's pounding on the bathroom door.

There's nowhere for me to run. My belongings are all downstairs, including my mobile – who would I call anyway? Staying in here will only make him furious, and my punishment more severe.

Shivering with fear, I walk back out; he's on the sofa masturbating, waiting.

'Turn around! I don't want to see your ugly face.'

I get down on the carpet, turning the other way so he won't see my face.

'Useless little slut, disgusting bitch ...' he carries on humiliating me with his horrible words.

Abruptly he stands up. When I look back he is already

Cleaning and Hoovering

lifting something that looks like a horsewhip; it comes down so hard I cannot even scream. He whips me continuously, on my back, bottom and legs.

'Keep still, bitch, or I will tie you up.'

I'm moving around on the floor, crying wretchedly. As the beating continues, so my tears become more anguished. Soon I realise that it is not only the awful pain that is making me cry – it's something deeper. I'm shedding tears for all my sorrows. I'm thinking of my miserable situation, all those job rejections, being unemployed with no place in society, having absolutely no one I can turn to. The flow of depressive feelings is magnified by the barrage of his abusive words:

'Fucking useless bitch. You should bury yourself to make the world a better place. You are good for nothing. You don't deserve to exist. Your only function is to be beaten ...'

I think about my grandmother who died last year. I can see myself standing there at the cemetery during the ceremony. I loved her more than anything else in the world; and she adored me, always proud of how well I did at school. But what would she think of me now? *Nanna, please forgive me. Nanna, you should never have been so proud ...*

How ironic that I should be here – the good girl who never got into trouble, who kept to herself and concentrated on her studies. All the usual teenage experiences I missed out on – boozy nights, experimenting with drugs, dating guys, losing your virginity – and now I'm twenty-four and still none of these things has yet to happen. I thought that if I moved abroad, away from my safe but boring cocoon, then finally I would grow up. However, instead of being in the middle of freedom, it feels more like the middle of nowhere ... *he continues to masturbate while whipping me all over my body, obtaining great pleasure in my pain and tears* ... So is this the real life I was longing for? Am I now a real adult? Or does my pain signify that no matter whether I live with my family or move abroad to start a new life, I will always stay the same worthless girl? He confirms these doubts while whipping me:

'You are a *useless* little slut. Do you understand?'

Now he begins to use a thick cane. The pain is becoming incredible. I'm moving around the floor, trying to avoid the touch of it. My disobedience makes him roar.

'Keep still you fucking bitch!'

I'm crying desperately, begging him to stop, but he keeps on hitting me. I feel completely empty inside. I close my eyes as I don't want to see the outside world any more, and I enter a new dimension that I've never experienced. There is no space, no time, no need for mercy or help. Just close my eyes and the world around me disappears. I'm realising my function: a 'useless' object, grumbling in pain, swimming in my own tears that at least provide pleasure to someone. Now I can enjoy the tears as they splash down my face, into my mouth and ears, moistening my neck and hair. What a relief to be

Cleaning and Hoovering

crying out all my sorrows …

He pulls me by the hair, throwing me into his desired position, then cuffs my hands and feet. He begins beating me again with all his strength. When he has had enough he watches me as I writhe on the floor, and masturbates, taking pleasure in my pain … But even after so long, his orgasm will not come.

Infuriated, he takes off his trousers.

'Now I'm going to rape you, slut.'

I look at him in terror … I'm screaming madly, making clumsy movements in the cuffs, trying desperately to escape.

'… *Good girl!*' he screams in relief. Seeing me there, entirely powerless and helpless, is enough to finally bring about his long-awaited pleasure.

I'm on the floor, feeling exhausted from pain and terror. After he has finished cleaning himself he takes off the cuffs and drops a couple of notes onto my body.

'You're lucky today,' he says, grinning.

I do not even move. All I do is gaze down at my stockings which are now full of holes.

1

Job-Search Misery

Finally I am sitting on the train. My mum and little sister are on the platform. They're waving to me. My mum is crying; I can see the tears as they roll down her face, her facial expression revealing all her fears and worries. Though I am an adult, she still thinks of me as a child, and that's one of the reasons I have decided to move abroad and start a new life.

My big blue suitcase is beside me. It's all I will possess in my new world — an idea which both scares and excites me. I imagine that it will be like on films: the poor girl from the little village arrives with nothing, yet finds luck and happiness in her new land. But my vivid dreams are interrupted by a bitter feeling of guilt as I look outside the window and see my sobbing mother. I cannot wait for the train to depart. I do not want to see her

Job-Search Misery

tears. I do not wish to feel guilt. I would like to leave it all behind.

My heart beats faster as I hear the engine, the train is ready to leave. My mum's tears multiply but I see less of them as the train moves ahead. My family is disappearing in the distance, though I can still hear my mum screaming 'take care of yourself. We love you,' her voice soon swallowed by the miles.

I'm lying in bed, thinking how it's now been three long weeks and still I'm without a job. I'm beginning to wonder about the whole idea of finding one – is there even any reason for me to get out of bed? ... *Hey, don't dig yourself into a pit of self-indulgence. You need to keep searching; don't give up now. You've got to prove that you can find work in the capital of England. You are in London! IN LONDON, DO YOU UNDERSTAND! In one of the coolest and most significant places in the world. Everyone else is working, you are not any worse than them. Get up and hunt, like a tiger in the jungle!*

I climb out of bed and begin to prepare myself, trying to achieve a presentable look so I don't scare off any employers. Anyway, at 3pm I have a second interview for a waitress position in a nice posh hotel – at least they must have been impressed, or they would not have called me back.

The interview goes well – at least I thought it did; however, in a few days I receive the usual apologetic letter in a smart envelope 'regretting' to inform me that I have

On Undefended Flesh

not been successful, stressing how they have had such an 'overwhelming number of responses from high-calibre applicants with more experience'. Oh yes, silly me, how dare I apply for such a prestigious position! Hadn't they read my letter where I clearly stated that though I possess enthusiasm, energy, and a great willingness to acquire new skills, I do not have any waitressing experience? So why were they playing with me? And to top it off, like some cruel hoax, I have to receive the letter on my birthday.

I try to stay calm and optimistic. Even if it's all a big challenge, there's also the thrill of being completely alone in a foreign country. There is no one I can rely on except myself, and I will have to fight in every way. But there's also the exciting opportunity to rebuild my whole life, to become the person I've always wanted to be.

I cannot surrender to my bad luck, and I decide to change tactics. Instead of copying countless numbers of my CV each day, distributing them among the shops and restaurants as I walk up and down the streets, and getting nowhere, I now go down to the internet café and post ads on websites, under the 'Looking for Work' category. Though I have been advised to embellish my work experience with pleasing lies, I find that I cannot give a false impression of myself, and perhaps that is my downfall.

Job-Search Misery

So again, today, I create another one of my sincere ads:

LET ME GET OUT OF MY JOB-SEARCH MISERY
I am a nice, well-mannered girl who is desperately seeking a sensible, full-time job. I am willing to work as much as possible with great flexibility regarding the working hours. I am happy to work as part of a team as well as taking my own initiative.

I do not have too much work experience but am eager to learn new skills and broaden my mind with relevant knowledge. I was an English language teacher in my home country. I moved to London as I thought it was the land of opportunities with lots of job vacancies, but soon realised that it is already full, and now am struggling to find a job.

Please call or text me on _____
I am looking forward to your reply.

I receive a few phone calls from pubs and restaurants, but when I tell them that I do not have any references or experience in hospitality they quickly lose interest. Thankfully, I manage to secure an interview at a small company who are looking for an office cleaner ... All seems well; however, the next morning the manager phones me, saying he thinks I'm 'too intelligent' for such a job ... *Now I really feel like screaming!* All I want is to be accepted as a real citizen of my chosen country, contributing to it with all my heart. I'm willing to start

On Undefended Flesh

from the bottom, cleaning, serving, etc. I only ask for a chance.

It's no comfort when my mother calls, as I have to confess that even after all these weeks I am still jobless. She must think that I will soon give up and run home, like when I first went to university on the other side of the country, only to return home after a week. But I need to prove to myself and my mother, I am able to live a life and support myself.

2

Funny Business in Brighton

I keep on posting my ads on the Internet. Most of the responses seem dodgy, but one does manage to intrigue me.

> *Hi,*
> *I have a vacancy for an honest and reliable girl to join my existing escort team. THERE IS ABSOLUTELY NO SEX OR TOUCHING INVOLVED! All training will be provided. Earn £70 per hour (paid daily) for film work and sessions. Work in either London or Brighton. A great opportunity for the right girl to earn loads of money. Call me on _____ for a chat.*
>   *Milo@*

On Undefended Flesh

The hourly rate is incredible, but I'm concerned with the term 'escort' as I've always heard it in reference to prostitution – which is the one thing I would never do.

Finally I decide to give Milo a call to find out exactly what it is. When he answers the phone he tells me about a bizarre 'adult school' he runs, where men pay to spank women dressed as schoolgirls on the bottom. He assures me the spanking is in no way severe and that there is nothing sexual about it. I'm reluctant, considering what happened last time. However, as each day goes by, my bank balance is heading closer towards zero – and I'm getting more desperate ...

*

I catch the train down to Brighton. Milo's there waiting at the station – an energetic, friendly-looking guy around forty. We begin walking to his school, but as we pass the sea we stop for a while to admire the view.

'It's beautiful!' I say aloud. Though the day is cold, the sun is out and the water looks mesmerising.

He waits patiently while I take in this rare sight.

We continue walking, eventually ending up at a run-down terrace apartment. Leading me to a room, he shows me a selection of school uniforms from which I have to choose. As I've never worn one before (they are not used at all in my country), I can't help feeling a little excited. I put on a shirt, cardigan, skirt and a pair of long, white socks that reach my knees. I put my hair into bunches, and when I check the mirror I feel I have transformed into a real English schoolgirl.

'That's great! I think that is your colour, green. It suits you perfectly,' Milo says, looking pleased. 'I'm guessing you will be very popular with the clients.'

'Don't flatter me,' I say, smiling.

'Now that Martina has left, I need a new girl who can replace her. Who can be as brilliant as her, or even better.'

'Martina?'

'Yes, a Polish girl who worked with me for two years. She earned so much money she moved back to Poland and bought a house there.'

He sets up the camera and lighting for the video, and instructs me on how to pose. I have to bend over a proper school bench, kneel down on pencils scattered on the floor (which is surprisingly quite painful!), stand in a corner, and also stand in front of a giant map of the world that is meant to give the room an authentic classroom look.

While recording, he comes up to me and spanks my bottom. He becomes quite upset when he notices all the markings on my thighs. (Though it has now been one week since that horrible night, many of the marks are still visible.)

'This is not proper training – but torture!' Milo says. 'I've trained over fifty women on the art of being a submissive, and none of it involved this.'

On Undefended Flesh

I keep silent, not sure how to respond.

'How much did he pay you?' he continues.

'Twenty pounds.'

He starts shaking his head in disbelief. 'Please, come work for me. You will earn a lot more money with only a fraction of the pain. But you have to promise me to not see men like this, we can't risk it.'

We continue with the filming. As he spanks me, he focuses the camera on my face so that all my emotions and reactions will be seen. He seems very satisfied with me; I'm enjoying it as well (the video being more cheeky fun than a torture session), so much so that at one point I burst out laughing. His face, however, suddenly becomes stricter, and he begins to smack me harder in order that I cry – only a tear, but enough to add something to the film.

When he has finished filming, Milo leaves the room and goes to his office. Soon someone arrives for a session with me. The client is probably in his fifties – a short, fat man with greying hair, who looks a little unkempt. He seems embarrassed, and tells me that he has never done anything like this before. The session is rather awkward as he wants me to take charge; but I have no idea how to entertain a man who does not know what he wants. He spanks me for a while on my bottom, then I crawl around on the floor and watch him masturbate, feigning interest. Time is passing by extremely slowly and I can't wait for the session to finish. In the end he leaves before the sixty minutes are up.

Milo is cross when I tell him what happened, and assures me that there is never any masturbation, only playful discipline scenarios with plenty of spanking by clients who know exactly what they want. After I have gotten dressed and am ready to leave, he hands me an incredible £150 cheque for the video and £70 cash for the one-on-one, adding that he would like to work with me on a regular basis. He says he's impressed with my submissive skills and wants to make a new film with me in the countryside: running in the fields with different school uniforms, confessing my sins, asking for severe punishment, and other such things.

We say goodbye to each other, promising to keep in touch.

*

Hi Shana,
You were brilliant yesterday, thanks for making my day. Hopefully you can sit down without too much pain.

As I told you yesterday, I am sure I will be able to find you plenty of work because you are such a beautiful, genuine person. It will be a pleasure to train you and show you the true art of being a submissive, to make sure you become the very best.
Milo@

On Undefended Flesh

Unfortunately Milo turns out to be unreliable, and a few days later I receive another email:

Hi Shana,
Sorry to have to tell you this, but I've decided to close down my school. I have had some trouble with my business partners, as well as being sued by a girl who appeared in one of my films. I will not forget you, and as soon as I've sorted everything out I will get back to you with work.
Take care.
Milo@

3

Going Professional

Now that I can't rely on Milo anymore – and realising that there is plenty of money to be made from this bizarre pastime – I decide to post a new ad on the Internet (this time under an *entirely* different category).

Nice young innocent submissive girl is available for beating and humiliation. Sexual touching is excluded.

The following evening when I check for responses, I'm amazed to find my inbox flooded with over one hundred emails. I begin reading them:

When I saw your ad I really focused on the word

On Undefended Flesh

submissive. I'm a very open-minded guy who likes to dominate. I'll use all types of implements on you, but my favourite is my hand, as I like to feel a girl's flesh with it. I'm really into teasing and denying orgasm till you beg for it. I'd try outdoor sex, though as I'm not an exhibitionist I wouldn't want to get caught. My picture is in the attachment, and if you like what you see don't hesitate to get back to me.

____@

Just got out of jail and I'm crazy for some female action. Only thing I want is that you are shaved, because I'm going to be spending a lot of time down there if you know what I mean. I really enjoy receiving too, but you better do it right or you will be punished.

____@

You're a lucky girl. A vacancy has just opened up as one of my school sex slaves. I am Nick, 29, and I am a particularly dirty headmaster. You will learn things that you were never taught at school. So if you have a uniform, apply within, for a good caning followed by a severe fucking.

____@

Didn't I clearly state nothing sexual? As I skim through the rest of the responses I realise they are all the same: men who want some form of perverted, sexual pleasure.

Going Professional

However, I do come across one email which at least might prove helpful:

Hi,

You need to be careful babe, as most men would not allow you to dictate the terms of the meeting so rigidly. Excluding sex could be dangerous as it will only breed frustration and anger, also there is the very real possibility that you will meet a truly sick person who will violate you against your will. I myself would only agree to meet if you offer, at the very least, mutual masturbation, since men need some kind of sexual reward.

I will teach you everything there is to know about the art of submission, as I am a master with 20 years experience. I am into all forms of BDSM, including caning, figging, bondage, fisting and electrosex. (Yes, I do have all the equipment!) I will be your master, confidante and teacher.

Be aware that I never pay! Why would I, when I can meet so many educated women who do it for free. If you are an amateur whore, I suggest a better and safer option is to go to www._____ This a free website for both spankee and spankers to advertise.

Remember, there is nothing better in life than to please one's master. Get back to me.

Marcus@

On Undefended Flesh

Going to the spanking website he suggested, I place an advert, modelling it on other ads that I see there:

NICE YOUNG SUBMISSIVE GIRL AVAILABLE
She is obedient, humble, naughty, and cheeky. After a comprehensive spanking, caning, humiliation, she is able to behave as a good girl. She is especially keen on being verbally and mentally humiliated, but she is well aware of the fact that physical pain is also essential for her to become a good girl. She loves pleasing her masters. She is very broad-minded but innocent and pure as well. She needs strict, experienced masters who will punish her in London.
SHANA SHINE

Hi Marcus,
I am so grateful to you. This website is a real goldmine for me. I have received plenty of responses to my ad, and we have the mutual interest that they are willing to pay and do not require sex. The whole submissive thing came to me by accident, not realising how spanking is such a big subculture in Britain. Being a submissive is very easy for me because I am humble and obedient by nature; but I have to charge money, as first, I really need some, and second, I think it is only fair to receive compensation for the sometimes severe physical pain. Though I know it is dangerous to visit men in their private apartments, I have to admit I do

Going Professional

get a thrill out of it, even if I do not enjoy the pain.
It will be a bit difficult to organise the bookings ...
Thanks again for the website suggestion.
Shana@

Hi Shana,
No doubt you have had many responses by now. But
be warned, most of them will be timewasters — men
who are inexperienced and don't have the balls to go
through with it. Others will be genuine, and then there
will be the psychos — and remember, even a submissive
should value their life. I've used the website before and
it's a real lottery who you will end up with.
Marcus@

Meanwhile, I receive a phone call from a huge department store in central London, inviting me in for an interview.

Having arrived early, I stand at the entrance of the grand building, waiting for the interview to start. I have no retail experience, nor any interest or knowledge concerning the sports products that they sell, so I do not harbour any naïve hopes, just attend the interview as part of my daily routine.

The manager is nice and friendly, though her smile is suspiciously wide as we sit down to talk. Having become somewhat immune to all the rejections by now, I do not stress at all, not expecting anything anyway.

On Undefended Flesh

'Well then, I would like you to join our team,' she says after asking me only a few questions, her smile becoming even wider. 'It will be a full-time position. Can you start tomorrow?' When she hands me a piece of paper with the word *Congratulations* clearly visible, it really sinks in that I have got a job, and I am overwhelmed with joy.

The induction goes well (too many bits of information, too many new people – but I think I will cope) and they place me in men's footwear. There are hundreds of shoes everywhere, each with a different name, colour and size. There are also strict rules such as no chatting with colleagues and no standing around, as well as long working hours; but at least my mind is occupied, and there is no time for any depressing thoughts. I try to always serve the customers with a friendly smile, and usually they reward me with a big 'thank you'.

My mum is not too happy when she hears I am serving shoes and packing boxes with my teacher's qualification. In any case, if I compare my less classy shop-assistant position with my experience as a teacher, I can only feel relief. One has to be born a teacher – it is like being on stage; and though I love the English language, I was neither able to maintain my students' attention nor discipline. My family kept telling me slowly-by-slowly I would get used to it, yet in the end I never did. So what a relief I won't be returning to teaching … and now I know I won't have to return back home.

4

My Chelsea Master – Part 1

It's so nice to come home after a particularly busy day in the store. I'm so looking forward to a relaxing hot bath; I'm just about to step in when my mobile beeps.

/Saw ad on _____. Am very interested. Live in Chelsea. Can I call to discuss?/

Brief, but to the point – like a man who knows what he wants. And *Chelsea?* Isn't that the posh part of town? Hoping for the best I send him my now standard reply:

/I am a nice young virgin submissive. You can beat and humiliate me because I deserve it.

On Undefended Flesh

The only limit is sexual touching. I know that I am a worthless piece of shit. You can call me to talk details./

The prospect of a new, rich client is enticing, but I'm also dead tired. I'm in the bath, yawning, eyes drooping, wondering when he will call. I'm dozing by the time he finally does.

'Hallo,' he says, in a surprisingly soft voice. 'I saw your advert and I'm very interested. I respect your limits and assure you I do not want to have sex with you – I just want to beat and humiliate you.' He pauses. 'So tell me about yourself. How did you end up as a sub?'

I begin telling him about my move from Hungary, how I stumbled into the sub world through my job adverts on the Internet, and a little bit about my experience so far – all through which he listens intently.

'So what would you do with me exactly?' I ask.

'I will humiliate you verbally, beat you extremely hard, and cane you brutally.'

'How many strokes?'

'Let's say one hundred for a start.'

I'm silent, stunned by the amount.

'One hundred cane strokes,' he continues. 'Are you able to take it?'

'Yes, of course,' I reply coolly, hoping to convince myself as much as him. My first pay packet will not be arriving for another three weeks, and no matter how

My Chelsea Master – Part 1

painful, I need to grab this opportunity with both hands. I steer the conversation towards my overriding issue.

'You do know that I'm commercial?'

'Yes, I thought as much. How much do you charge?'

'How much would you pay?' thinking it best to answer with a question. Though in the past I have generally found rich people to be quite stingy, you just never know ...

'I was thinking six hundred pounds.'

There is a striking silence from both ends of the line. *Did I really hear that ... six hundred! Think of how many hours I would need to sell shoes ...*

'Well, that sounds fair,' I say, trying hard to disguise my excitement.

'Good. I'll text you when and where.'

A few minutes later I receive the details:

/_____ **Road, SW3. Wednesday 4pm**/

I'm both terrified and elated. How painful will one hundred strokes be? Would someone really pay that much money just to beat and humiliate someone?

He sends another text:

/**You will be put in your place next Wednesday. You will be dragged around by your hair, beaten hard and receive severe markings. You will cry a lot. You will be**

treated like the worthless piece of shit you are./

This guy sounds really serious. I think I can handle the pain, but what if he tries to rape me? I send him a text to make sure, to which he promptly replies:

/I won't touch you. I'm not interested in your worthless body. I am your master and you are my slave. My property. Don't be late./

That night I can't sleep, I'm tossing and turning thinking about next week. Over the following days, whether I'm at home or at work, a hundred questions absorb me. What is his house like? What if he can't control himself? Do his neighbours live close enough to hear me scream? And of course, those one hundred cane strokes …

*

It's Wednesday, 17th May, and the bus arrives at King's Road. I'm busy concentrating on where to get off, constantly glancing between my map and the street signs. Everywhere are beautiful buildings, elegant shops and restaurants, and well-dressed, snobby-looking people. I step off the bus and make haste. I'm desperate for a pee but don't dare stop; if I am late it will only mean more punishment, and four o'clock is fast approaching. Only when I am within a few houses of his do I slow down,

My Chelsea Master – Part 1

my heart now beating out of my body. I look up at the magnificent building and ring the bell. *Now there is no turning back.*

'Hallo.'

'Hi, it's me. The slave.'

The door opens and there he is: a man in his late forties, average height and a little chubby – not too charming at first sight. He motions for me to come in. He does not say anything, just stares at me, inspecting me. But I have to break the silence with an urgent plea:

'May I go to the toilet please?' Having not forgotten my first master, I am prepared for any response.

'Yes, you may. The bathroom is over there.' He points to one of the numerous doors while I sigh in relief.

As I enter the bathroom the lights switch on automatically, fascinating me; *how do they do that?* I sit there on the toilet, taking in my sumptuous surroundings. Everything looks immaculate and shining.

When I return I stand in front of him. He reaches into his pocket.

'Here is some money for the school uniform you must buy from Peter Jones.'

'Who is Peter Jones?'

He looks at me incredulously.

'It's the huge department store in Sloane Square. Didn't you see it as you were coming?'

I shake my head. I would like to tell him that I was a little too preoccupied with thoughts of what will happen here today to be regarding the names of stores I couldn't afford to shop in anyway.

'It has a schoolwear department. You need to buy a proper school uniform, including a grey pleated skirt, white shirt, knee-length socks and proper school panties. You can choose the items on your own so it will be a surprise for me.'

I'm left completely bewildered by his list.

'Could you come with me? I don't know where to find this store and have no idea what you would like.'

He seems reluctant.

'Just this once,' he finally agrees, annoyed.

We walk along. He seems rigid and cold, not saying a word. It begins to rain. He opens his umbrella and holds it over him, while I follow a few paces behind in the rain, like a dog – or a slave, to be precise. Water splashes down my face, over my body. The awkward silence is more discomforting however; but I have nothing to say and neither it appears does he. Perhaps there is no need to say anything anyway.

We arrive at an impressive building of shining glass, full of elaborate displays in the windows. While we are in the lift I realise it will be quite odd for someone my age to be browsing for school uniforms.

'What will the shop assistants think? It will be embarrassing.'

'You can tell them you're going to a fancy dress party,'

My Chelsea Master – Part 1

he replies calmly.

We reach the fourth floor and walk through the toys department.

'OK, I'll wait here. Choose something nice that you think I would like.'

Feeling self-conscious, I browse through the skirts, trying to keep as far away from the shop assistants as possible. *Just leave me alone and I will find for myself what I am looking for ...* But what am I looking for exactly? How am I supposed to know what he would like?

I decide to sort out this awkward shopping list as quickly as possible. Not daring to go to the fitting room, I pick up one of the larger grey skirts, too embarrassed to even measure it by holding it to my waist. I grab a white blouse with the same haste. Now only the socks and panties. *Oh, my God! Panties!* The most embarrassing item, and they just happen to be right up near the counter, where all the salespeople are.

'May I help you?' An enthusiastic shop assistant looks up at me.

'No, thanks. I'm just ... *(what shall I say? 'Going to a fancy dress' – it sounds fake!)* looking for some stuff for ... *(for what? For something to wear while I receive a hundred lashes!)* I'm just looking thanks.' I pull a fake smile as my face burns up; I know I must be as bright as a tomato right now. I give up on buying school panties and head straight for the counter. Recognising some socks, I throw a pair into my basket and the cashier

On Undefended Flesh

proceeds to scan my items.

My Chelsea master is standing further along, trying to look inconspicuous as he talks to someone on his phone. I hand him the change and receipt. By the time we are outside he is still on the phone, discussing business. I don't understand the conversation, but just walk after him in the rain, thinking of the brutal moments that await me. He is not friendly or kind, and I can expect the worst. Perhaps he may turn out to be even crueller than my first master, if that is at all possible.

When we get back to the house he realises he has left his keys inside.

'This has never happened to me before. This is all your fault.'

'I know,' I say, trying to reassure him.

He looks irritated as he phones someone.

'Come on, slave, I'll have the key in twenty minutes. We're going to the pub now. You walk after me.'

A few minutes later we arrive at a nice English pub, but I'm not allowed in.

'Stay out here in the rain and wait for me.'

It's raining, not so heavily now but I feel it moistening my skin. I begin to feel humiliated, though I shouldn't be surprised as this is the type of service I am offering. Anyway, perhaps there is nothing more rewarding than standing outside a pub, like a dog waiting for its owner.

Thirty minutes later he comes out.

'We can go now.'

My Chelsea Master – Part 1

When we are close to his place he tells me to stay. 'I'll call you when you can come.' He must not want me to be seen by the locksmith. I can see him in the distance receiving a key from a young guy, and a couple of minutes later he phones me.

'Now you'll get dressed in this room, then wait till I come.'

I throw my stuff into a corner and start to get dressed, wondering if I will even fit into these clothes designed for schoolgirls. I squeeze myself into the shirt and skirt – somehow they fit perfectly.

Waiting for him, I sit down on the floor and gaze about the room. An abstract painting of a fat couple eating breakfast hangs above, its freakish quality making the occasion feel more ominous. A gigantic bookshelf nearby is crammed full of books. I stare up at the titles but am in such a state of anticipation that I can see nothing. And now I hear him coming –

'Stand up!'

He looks me over, paying particular attention to my legs.

'Come upstairs.'

When we reach the staircase he grabs my hair (just like he mentioned in one of his texts), pulling me up like an object. He drags me into a spacious room. The huge TV is on, and he sits down. I have to stand there next to him while he stares at me. I can feel his eyes on my bones, checking out my figure and my slave compatibility.

'You're a worthless piece of shit, you know that? Why have you come here?'

'Because I know I am worthless and deserve the severe punishment you promised me.'

'What kind of punishment is it going to be?'

'Hard caning,' I reply with a sad sigh.

'How hard, you dirty piece of shit?' His voice is getting louder.

'One hundred strokes.'

'Are you prepared to take all those cane strokes?' he asks, a grin on his face.

'Yes, I am. Because I want to be a good girl.'

'Good! Now get down on your knees and crawl around the table.'

I get on my hands and knees, and do a lap around the coffee table.

'Shall I do it again?'

'Did I tell you to stop, *slave*!' he responds angrily.

I carry on with the crawling.

'Faster! *Faster!*' he demands.

I crawl as fast as I can, the whole thing making me feel like I'm back at school in some twisted physical education class.

'Enough! Stand up!' He looks at my red knees. 'Now crawl to the corner and think about your sins and misdeeds.'

I make the mistake of taking my first step on my feet, having not heard him properly.

My Chelsea Master – Part 1

'I said CRAWL!' he screams out like a man possessed.

'Now stand up with your head down, legs apart, feeling ashamed. Take off your panties.'

'But it's too embarrassing!' I protest.

'*I decide everything. You have no say, you are a slave.* Do you understand?'

Reluctantly I pull down my panties.

It becomes tiresome standing there for a long time without movement. Sometimes I steal an inquisitive glance to the shelves, to see photos of smiling children. *Could they really be his?*

'I said head facing the floor!' he yells.

'Lift your skirt up and show me your bare bottom.'

I do as I'm told. In another context it could be quite funny: standing in a corner with my skirt raised. But not this one – I'm too scared to be feeling the bizarre.

'You are nothing. You are less than the dirt on my shoes. You deserve to be treated like the little piece of shit you are. Don't you?'

'You're right,' I reply, 'there is no proper word to describe how worthless I am.'

'You shouldn't have been born to this planet.'

'That's true. It's a shame I was born at all.'

'You are a worthless object. You are not worth anything. You don't deserve anything apart from a severe beating.'

His words begin to pierce me and I feel so small, so

miserable ... *so worthless*. Tears roll down me and I'm getting wet — not just my face but down there as well. I'm so ashamed.

'May I have your permission to go to the bathroom?' I ask as politely as I can, desperate to clean myself up.

'Why?'

'I have to pee.'

'Again?' He sounds suspicious.

'Yes, again,' I beg for his mercy.

'Go then!'

I would run downstairs immediately if I did not remember where I was. Instead, feeling immensely relieved by this 'favour', I get down on my hands and knees and crawl to the stairs. When I am halfway down, I crouch on my feet; I must be silent — I do not even dare imagine his anger if he should catch me not crawling. Only when I am near the bottom do I stand upright and run.

Inside the bathroom I realise just how wet I have become, needing plenty of tissues to wipe myself dry. Why is this happening? I am not attracted to him. It's perplexing but there is no time to dwell on it. Cautiously I tiptoe back to the top of the staircase, before resuming the proper slave position and crawling into the room.

'Now stay down on your knees and crawl around the table again.'

He makes me stop when I am near his feet.

'You're going to be my footstool.' He puts his feet on my back and carries on watching television.

My Chelsea Master – Part 1

'You're not good enough to be my footstool. You're so worthless, useless, despicable. Aren't you?'

'I am.'

It becomes really uncomfortable after a while. His legs are so heavy and my back is beginning to ache. I'd like to move just a little bit to ease the pain.

'Don't move!' he shouts, kicking me angrily.

His mobile rings and he begins talking to a woman called Jennifer, who must be his secretary. They're having a long conversation concerning business, all through which I am underneath his legs, his heavy shoes on my back, and he acting as though it were the most trivial thing in the world to be talking on the phone while having some human under your feet.

After the conversation finishes he orders me to go upstairs with him. It proves quite challenging on my hands and knees, crawling up steep steps as he yanks me up by my hair. Finally, after a difficult journey, we arrive at the upper floor and enter his bedroom. It's a beautiful sunlit room, with a big bed that is covered by a snow-white duvet, and plenty of photos of those same kids I saw in the living room. There is also a nice photo of him kissing a woman. *He must be a romantic!* But right now he is staring at me with merciless eyes as he towers above me.

'Bend over my knees and I will spank your bare bottom.'

I bend over his lap and he begins spanking me with

strong hands. It is quite painful though not enough to make me cry – but I know I need not wait too long for tears.

'Now get into position on the bed,' he says.

'Which position?'

'Bend over on the bed, kneeling. Your bottom exposed, skirt lifted up.'

It dawns on me suddenly that when I was caned by my first master, I at least had panties and stockings on. What kind of pain will I have to endure without even light clothing for protection?

'You'll receive your punishment in stages. You'll get a break after every twenty-five strokes.' He looks at me as though he was being too generous.

He walks over to the wardrobe to select some canes, whisking them deftly through the air like a man familiar with his tools, all the while maintaining that same rigid, cold expression.

'You'll say thank you after every stroke and count them out aloud.'

Tensing up, I try to stay strong. I think about the money, hoping it will give me strength, repeating the digits *six, zero, zero* in my head. But all thoughts are cast aside when the first stroke lands on my flesh; it is so fierce! I scream out immediately.

The pain, however, only seems to grow with each successive stroke. I am crying and screaming as the cane cuts my thighs. He's not interested in my bottom, only my thighs – he knows it is more painful. He cuts every part of them, moving about the bed to get the best angle, not wanting any part to remain pure. The physical pain becomes unbearable. I cannot keep still, turning my head to the left and right, wanting to see where the next stroke is coming from. I want to prove that I can take the whole punishment, but it's only the tenth stroke and I find myself begging for a break.

'You've had only ten. You've got ninety left. Do you understand?'

I bury my face in the pillow but it does not help. I try to conjure up a scene where I am happy and relaxed, everyone loves me, the sun is shining, birds are singing, flowers are blooming ... but it is all being washed away by my tears.

I cannot stop crying and screaming. I'm actually quite disappointed with my performance, I just would never have believed that it could hurt so much. And the counting only makes it worse. Each time I say a number I realise just how many there are to go. It is only the seventeenth, but I already feel as though I am unable to continue. I move away, crying desperately. But he is not sympathetic, telling me to be a good girl and get back into position.

'Three more, then you can have a break after the twentieth.'

Knowing that there are only three gives me the strength to make it to twenty. I get up off the bed and

On Undefended Flesh

try to walk; my thighs are on fire, cut and bruised all over. I blow my nose as it is blocked from all my crying. He asks me to get back on the bed so he can see all the bruises. I hope he's satisfied, but how can I do twenty more, let alone another *eighty*?

A couple of minutes later he wants me back in position. I place my head into the wet pillow. He's searching for a pure spot on my thighs, but it's not easy after twenty severe ones, so he goes further down, the implement catching me close to the knee. I move around and scream; even if he demands complete obedience it's the only way to release the pain, and soon I am crying and sobbing like before. *What is wrong with me today?* This is no worse than my torture with my first master, and here I am only a quarter way through, utterly exhausted.

'You'll have five more. Then you'll get a longer break.'

Thank God! Somehow I make it to thirty. I jump up from the bed like a crazed woman, walking around deliriously, collapsing to the floor when I realise it won't alleviate the pain I am suffering. I lay there lifeless, no strength or energy to stand on my feet, crying. Chelsea Master is sitting on the sofa with his belt off, grabbing his penis and rubbing it.

'Kneel down beside the sofa and cry for me.'

I lean against the sofa as he enjoys the sight of my tears. His cock is in front of me, though I'm too exhausted to care and by now am used to the sight of men touching

My Chelsea Master – Part 1

themselves. I stare straight through him, sapped of all energy, yet still managing to give the impression I am interested in what he is doing. Though I try I cannot stop crying, but at least my tears seem to turn him on, and the sooner he gets his satisfaction the sooner I can stop pretending I'm fascinated with what he is doing. He gets more excited, his breathing becomes faster, and ...

He rests, basking in his pleasure which seems considerable, while I bury my head into my hands, contemplating the rest of my punishment. But suddenly I recoil: he's kicking into me – my legs, back, arms, stomach – wherever I am exposed. I cry harder now because of the brutality of the act – because it is so cruel. I am twisting all over the floor, really like a 'worthless piece of shit'.

Eventually he stops. I am on the floor, silent, motionless, helpless, feeling extremely weak both physically and mentally.

'Take off your clothes.'

His voice is softer now.

I lift up my head. 'Everything?'

'Yes, *everything*.'

Staggering to my feet, I take off the white shirt that has become all creased, and then my skirt. I'm standing there with only my white socks on, the rest of my uniform abandoned on the carpet.

'Can I leave my socks on?'

'Yes, you can leave your socks on,' he grants my wish as he sits on the bed.

His eyes begin roaming my body. I feel utterly miserable and humiliated.

'Now I'm going to give you a bare bottom spanking across my knee. Come here and bend over.'

Getting over his knees I feel no fear; it does not matter anymore ... I do not care about anything. When he has finished he takes me into his arms, giving me a big hug. I lay there numb, like an object without heart or soul, while he holds my naked body. I do not put my arms around him, do not respond to his cuddle, but feel disgusted in his arms, especially when he starts stroking my back with his fingers.

'The first part of your punishment is over. You were a good girl, a very good girl. I'm very pleased. We can go downstairs for a rest.'

He's speaking to me so gently.

'Can I put my clothes on?'

'You can,' he replies, while leaving the room.

'Shall I walk or crawl?'

'You must *crawl* of course!' he cries out from the staircase.

After getting back into my uniform I begin to feel better, even if I miss my underwear which is still in the living room. I crawl down the steps. When I enter the living room on all fours, he is watching television.

'To the corner. Lift your skirt up and stay there, silent. Don't move.'

I feel dizzy standing there, head down to the floor,

My Chelsea Master – Part 1

while he admires my bruised body.

'You worthless piece of shit. Did you deserve the punishment you just had?'

'I did. It will make me a good girl.'

'It will take a long time until you become a good girl,' he says, 'though you've done quite well so far.'

Angry with myself when I realise I have become wet again, I meekly ask his permission to go to the toilet for the third time today.

'Yes, you may,' he says, a suspicious smile on his face.

Great! Now he thinks he's turned me on. I am really annoyed that he will think that. But why have I gotten so wet again? It must be this whole crazy situation: being in a strange place with a strange man, being beaten, all the adrenalin rushing through me. Not because I am aroused by him. I would never let that happen. *Never!*

The first thing I do in the bathroom is look over my bruised body, being not particularly surprised by the multicoloured display that greets me. Every inch of me seems to hurt – even my dried-up eyes are as sore as the rest of me. In agony I wipe myself clean over the toilet, wondering how I will manage at work over the following days.

After I crawl back into the living room, he makes me stay beside the sofa on my knees. I can see more of the room now; stylish white furniture, plasma TV, elegant curtains ... But my attention focuses on a weird painting

On Undefended Flesh

hanging from the wall: a curvaceous naked woman stands by a blackboard, her face covered by a white veil, waiting for the man next to her to cane her. *Chelsea Master must really love caning.*

He is sitting on the sofa, watching TV. My mind fills with questions as I watch him. Who is this strange man? What does he do? Does he have a family? He seems so lonely and sad. For the first time today I begin to see him not just as a brutal beast but also as a man.

'What do you do for a living?' I ask, curiosity overcoming fear.

'I own a big company. More than a thousand people work for me all over the world.'

Ah, I expected as much, a big boss who commands and controls others.

'Do you have a wife, kids?'

'I got divorced a couple of years ago. I've got two kids who live with their mum but visit often.'

'How often?'

'At least twice a week.'

He doesn't seem to mind my questioning, emboldening me somewhat.

'Are you lonely?'

'I'm not lonely at all,' he says, taken aback. 'I've got the kids, I've got girlfriends, I've had lots of women around. Perhaps for a few weeks after the divorce I felt a bit lost, but not now ... I have such a busy life.'

'You've got girlfriends?'

'Yes, I've got a few. For example, the Spanish one used to be our nanny, but my wife fired her for lighting a cigarette in front of the kids.'

'If you've got girlfriends, how come you want to see me?'

He looks at me mischievously and grins. 'Cause I like caning girls. I saw your ad and found it intriguing. It's as simple as that.'

'Did you beat your wife as well?'

'No, she wasn't into it.'

'Is that why you got divorced?'

'It might have been one of the reasons, among many others.'

'How long did you live together?' I'm acting like an intrusive journalist wishing to know every detail, wanting to find clues as to who he is, why he is.

'Eleven years.'

'Did you love her?'

'I did, possibly. But it's over.'

'How did you meet?'

'Stop it now! Too many questions. You have to take the next part of your punishment; you've had only thirty, am I right?'

'Yes, but I can't take any more. Just look at me!' I point at my bruised body. 'I can't believe that there is someone out there who can take one hundred strokes.'

'One of my old girlfriends could,' he says.

I look at him sceptically, sure he is only trying to

manipulate me into taking more.

'OK, I'll give you a choice. You can choose to stop now, I'd understand and still pay you, as I'm fair and keep my word. Or you can choose to have another thirty strokes, in which case I would see you again, perhaps regularly.'

I'm surprised by the way he is talking to me right now; it's as though he considers me not just a slave but a proper person. Also, I'm tempted by the offer of becoming his regular slave, knowing I would never again have the opportunity to make so much money so quickly. But I have to consider the consequences on my daily life. What if I'm thrashed to the point where I can't move? Who will look after me? I have no one.

'Obviously I don't deserve the whole amount since I was unable to keep my word. I'm really ashamed of that, but I simply cannot take any more.'

'Are you sure you want to stop now? Is this your final word?'

I nod my head, aware of my limits.

'I understand,' he says, looking upset.

I can see the time on his clock: 7pm.

'Well, I think I'd better go home now.'

'I would like you to stay, but I can't force you. We could watch spanking movies. We can have dinner together,' he says. 'Of course, you would have to eat from a dog bowl on the floor,' he adds matter-of-factly.

'That would be really nice,' I reply. 'But it's late now.

My Chelsea Master – Part 1

I have to go.'

I just want to get paid, go home, and have a long, long sleep. I don't want to waste anymore time with him – a boring, perverted businessman away from his family, isolated in this huge house.

'You could be my live-in slave. You could have your own room in the basement. If you follow me I'll show you the room,' he says enthusiastically.

Curiosity again gets the better of me. Wanting to see for myself this room designed for slaves, I follow him down to the basement. He leads me to a dark room that is sparsely furnished with only a wardrobe and bed.

'You have to sleep here naked,' he reveals.

'Are there any mice or rats in the room?'

'I don't think so, but I can get them in for you if you stay.'

'I'm sure you would.' I have a slight grin on my face, and he too now begins to smile, changing that rigid look into something more human. 'It's a really nice offer but I can't stay here tonight. Maybe next time.'

He looks at me with a sad face again before locking the door, and I follow him up to the kitchen where he begins counting the money.

'Here's the whole fee as promised.' He approaches me, his arm outstretched.

Out of nowhere, I start to cry, my emotions pouring out of me. Of course I'm overjoyed to be receiving such a large amount of money, as well as sheer relief that the

On Undefended Flesh

whole thing is finally over; but I also feel other emotions:

'I don't deserve it. I didn't take all the strokes. I wasn't good enough.' I can hardly speak as I struggle through my tears.

All my old feelings of worthlessness flood back to me. I promised something and didn't deliver, *so how can I deserve all this money?* His arm remains outstretched with the money, but I am so overcome I cannot reach for it.

He looks at me compassionately, putting the money into my bag. 'You were a good girl and I keep my word.'

'Thank you,' I say sincerely, while sobbing.

I'm leaning against the wall, trying to compose myself, wiping the tears off my face. I can feel his eyes roaming my body.

'Why don't you stay? I have this kink but I'm really just a normal guy.'

Are you? I think to myself when I hear this. How can it be normal to want to cause a girl so much pain? How could he possibly consider himself to be normal?

I go to the dining room to pack my things, putting the schoolgirl stuff into the Peter Jones bag. 'I'll leave the uniform here,' I tell him, placing it in a corner.

He leads me to the front door, we exchange a quick goodbye, and I become free once more. Though we were together for three hours, it felt more like a whole day. Outside I become fresh again as I walk in the rain, feeling

My Chelsea Master - Part 1

the water splash down my face and roll away my tears. *The sky has been sobbing just like me ... perhaps the clouds have just had a session with the sun.*

Despite everything that's happened, I'm so excited about the money I've received. Walking along, I hold the bag next to me, protecting it from everyone and anyone as if I was hiding something incredibly precious inside; all the while I imagine what it will be like to hold that awful lot of money in my hands.

I cannot wait any longer. Stepping to the side of the pavement, I open my bag. It is all in fifty pound notes, and I begin to count them; but instead of twelve I discover only ten. I must have made a mistake, so I recount the notes ... but yes, two are definitely missing. I search desperately through my bag. People walk by and I'm still there on the pavement, searching frantically. What if I dropped it along the way? I look around and behind me. No, it could not be possible, I was holding the bag so tight.

Hurriedly I close the bag when I recognise a familiar figure in the distance: a well-groomed middle-aged man with a glum face coming towards me. He hasn't seemed to have noticed me, just walks along with his eyes glued to the pavement. Now I shall ask him about the missing money – but a little voice inside is telling me how even five hundred pounds is a wonder for such a poor and miserable girl like me.

He looks momentarily startled when I stop him.

On Undefended Flesh

'Come back and stay for the night – please. You can do the shopping for me. We can watch videos.'

I shake my head. He does not say anything, only turns his head down with disappointment.

'Where are you going now?' I ask.

'To buy some food.'

He turns towards a grocery store and asks me again, almost begging, 'Stay, please!'

'I'm sorry,' I say, and keep going.

5

My Chelsea Master – Part 2

The following days go by in terrible pain, though I'd say it was worse after my first master's tortures.

Hi Marcus,
I am still alive. He was a real gentleman yesterday but I was a bad girl because I gave it up after 30 strokes, it was so painful. I felt unable to do more (possibly because my period is coming?) and he still paid me the whole amount of money. £600 for a session! He did not cane my bottom at all, only my thighs. He humiliated me properly. I was dragged around by my hair, verbal humiliation, etc. No sex at all. He even asked me to stay for the night or for longer to be his live-in slave.
Shana@

On Undefended Flesh

Hello Shana,
Just got back from a session with one of my favourite regulars. It was her birthday — we went out to lunch, then followed by 40 strokes (one for each year) to multiply orgasm, then electrosex, fisting and fucking. I'm so sleepy right now.

So you're alive, congratulations! And you couldn't take a century of strokes? If I was paying I'd have demanded my money back. He must be a fool with plenty of money to burn.

Yes, around the time of your period, tolerance decreases as your skin becomes thinner. You should consider his offer of becoming a live-in slave. If you do, he will have you, then you might grow up. You are a money-grubbing whore who does not understand that there is more to life — friends, art, literature, sex — and this will be your downfall.

I'm surprised he didn't tie you down, as naughty girls deserve to be punished. And they must take whatever punishment was agreed. Very poor performance on your part. You will be soundly caned.
Marcus@

The bruises disappear slowly. They're fading day by day.

/You must come to my place next Wednesday 3pm to receive your next punishment.

My Chelsea Master – Part 2

You deserve a more brutal beating. Am I right?/

I am so surprised he still wants to see me.

/I am more than happy to visit you again. You are absolutely right, I do deserve a severe punishment again. I want to be a good girl. Same fee?/

I play with the idea of meeting him on a regular basis, imagining how much money I could earn. It could be a fortune.

/Yes, same fee. You will be beaten brutally, you worthless piece of shit. You will cry a lot and beg for more. You will eat from a dog bowl in the middle of the kitchen floor./

/I realised at home you gave me only £500. Was that on purpose or by mistake?/

/It was meant to be £600. I don't know what happened. Next time I will give you the missing money. I want to beat you again./

(Is he an international businessman who can't count!)

On Undefended Flesh

*

The past few days I have been getting increasingly nervous and sensitive: my period must be on its way. Periods have always been such a terrible affair for me, leaving me in crippling pain and heavy blood loss. Counting down the days I realise it's due tomorrow, Monday, a couple of days before I could become so much richer. It never arrives on time so I try and stay optimistic.

On Monday I am really anxious. Though I'm at work, I run to the toilet as often as possible to put my mind at rest. The morning goes by and there is still nothing in my panties – but by the afternoon I feel an increasing pain in my stomach ... I try and convince myself that it is all in my imagination; *I'm thinking about it too much, that's why it's there.* But the pain doesn't slacken – it really is there! – and soon I have an appointment that I cannot keep with period pain and bloody underwear.

Now I feel something hot and wet in my underwear. I run to the toilet and lose all hope when I see the evidence.

> **/I am awfully sorry but my period has just arrived so I cannot meet you this Wednesday. Unfortunately I have no control over such a biological process. Hope you would be willing to see me another time./**

> **/I can still meet you. I will whip only the**

My Chelsea Master – Part 2

> **bottom part of your legs. But then I can pay you only half the amount./**

I'm disappointed when I read this. Perhaps he is not as generous as I thought.

> **/That's not fair. It would be better to postpone the session for next week when I am pure again. I would perform much better and you would be more pleased./**

> **/OK. Next week then. You will cry so much for your insolence./**

The next few days keep me suffering in pain, a pain that is in fact as hard to bear as my master's cane. I imagine a session, trying to cope with the twin burdens. He sends a text, giving me an idea:

> **/Your body is a canvas for me to paint on. The paint is your blood, the brush is the cane./**

*

The following week I visit my Chelsea master for our second session. Greeting me at the door he immediately puts some money into my hands.

'You will go to buy proper white knee-high socks. There is a small shop on King's Road which specialises in socks.'

I find the place easy enough, and instantly become fascinated. Who would believe that a shop could exist selling only socks? It's a tiny but lovely place with lots of socks arranged on the tables. There is a whole section only for white socks, from which I choose a pair that are plain and simple though still pleasing to the eye, and pay the friendly cashier.

I arrive back to find my uniform waiting for me in the dining room, hanging from the back of a chair. He does not bother to come down.

'Get changed, then come up,' he shouts from upstairs.

Well, at least I won't be getting dragged up by my hair. I dress into the white shirt, which is still all creased from last time, and into the skirt and my new smart socks. I walk upstairs to find him on the sofa, watching TV. He stares at me, looking impressed with the socks, and asks me to take a seat next to him. After handing him the change and receipt, I sit down, aware of the embarrassed look on my face; I still can't believe this is all really happening.

'I will give you a choice,' he says, looking at me seriously. 'The money is in the kitchen. You can go downstairs, count it, put it in your bag. There is this week's fee, plus the money you said was missing. You can choose to go home with the money, without being beaten; or come back and take the punishment, which will be very

My Chelsea Master – Part 2

severe. So the decision is yours – either to get money for nothing or receive a painful beating.'

I'm amazed when I hear this. What a proposition, earning all that money for nothing!

He is staring at me with wondrous eyes. 'Go to the kitchen and put the money in your bag. Then choose the option you prefer.'

I go downstairs. The money is there on the bench like he said, a small pile of fifty pound notes. I count them quickly and then check again ... yes, definitely seven hundred. Though I am close to the door I'm not tempted to leave. I bundle the money into my bag and return to him.

'I am prepared to take my severe punishment. I offer you my thighs and bottom for a brutal beating. I never accept money for nothing, that is my principle.'

'Good. I wanted to see if you really are a submissive. Now get down on your knees.'

He gets me to crawl several times around the coffee table, before giving me my traditional corner time, panties down, hands on head. We then go to his bedroom on the top floor and I get into position on the bed, ready for the caning. He hits me hard, not weakened by my tears; he asks me not to scream out (probably concerned by the neighbours), so I bite on the pillow instead. It's all very painful, though I think I am doing better now that my period is out of the way.

After ten strokes I receive a short break, wiping my

On Undefended Flesh

face and clearing my nose with tissues. I make it to thirty and am awarded a longer break. I get up from the bed and collapse on the floor, my thighs bruised all over. He proceeds to masturbate. When he has finished wiping himself clean we go down a level to the living room where I transform into his footstool.

'Go downstairs to the kitchen and make me a drink: half gin, half tonic, with four pieces of ice. Tonic and ice in the fridge, gin in the cupboard.'

'Can I walk or shall I crawl?'

'Such a stupid piece of shit for asking me such a pointless question,' he shouts, getting me to bend over his knees. He spanks my bottom hard for forgetting that a slave should only crawl.

It takes me a while to find what I need in the kitchen. Having no idea about alcohol, I deliberate on whether to pour the tonic first or the gin. Eventually I decide on the tonic, then pour in the gin, giving an extra helping in the hope he will get drunk and forget about the rest of my beating. I walk back with the full glass (surely he doesn't expect me to crawl?), but start to worry when I enter the room; what if he does not like it? What if I forgot something? *No!* I recall the ice as I hand him the drink. Perhaps he won't notice though, as he already seems tipsy.

'Where's the ice?' he asks angrily.

'I'm awfully sorry. I do apologise.'

He spanks me again, over his knees on my bare

My Chelsea Master – Part 2

bottom, for my mistake. Then I revert to being a footstool while he drinks and smokes. After around twenty minutes he orders me to make another drink. This time I do not forget the ice, and make sure there is a lot more gin in the glass than tonic. We start talking while he is drinking, my back still functioning as a stool for his feet.

'You could be my live-in slave. You would be beaten every single day and do the cleaning. Of course you would have some free time, days when you could go out, maybe study something. You'd come with me when I travel abroad. You would carry the heavy luggage as a proper servant, lick my shoes clean, serve me drinks and meals.'

'You would only get bored of me after a while,' I say.

'No, I would always find something new – different punishments, different scenarios.'

'Have you ever had a live-in slave?'

'Not yet. But I'd like to have one. Perhaps you could even have a proper slave contract.'

'You mean an official paper outlining the terms and conditions.'

'Yes, something like that.'

'Do you have a cleaner?'

'Yes, I have a housekeeper who comes everyday.'

'Does she also cook for you?'

'No, I quite like cooking myself.'

'That's good, as I can't cook at all.'

'You won't need to cook. You'll get moulded bread and water —'

'— from a dog bowl in the middle of the kitchen floor,' I add, remembering his text.

'Exactly!' he says, smiling. 'Now come here.' He motions for me to crawl closer. I'm sure he will soon slap me ... but he does not. Instead he strokes my hair gently as he looks into my eyes.

'Good girl. You can sit down next to me.'

He is acting all strange right now, so tender and kind. I sit beside him, moving closer and closer, until I find myself in his arms, not quite sure how it even happened or who took the initiative. This is the first time I have ever cuddled a man before, and though I'm nervous and ashamed by what is happening, it also feels so good.

He starts kissing my face; I respond and kiss his. He searches for my mouth, but I turn away, not allowing him to kiss me on the lips. He is kissing my neck, holding me tight, wrapping me around his arms.

'My little girl. You'll be my little girl and I'll be your Daddy.'

'But you wanted me to be your slave.'

'No, I don't want you to be my slave. You'll be my little girl. My lovely little girl. My worthless adopted daughter.'

'My Daddy,' I whisper softly into his ears, 'my Daddy.'

My Chelsea Master – Part 2

'My little girl. I will adopt you.'

'I am so ashamed. I have never done anything like this before. Now you must think I'm a slut.'

'No, you are my little girl.' He smiles, holding me tight, caressing my face.

My head starts spinning when I realise I'm cuddling a man who I call Daddy … who is old enough to be my father. What's more, he beats me brutally and treats me like a piece of shit; and now I'm in his arms seeking his affection and enjoying these tender moments. *But what am I doing? Have I gone mad?*

'Why don't you kiss me?' he asks, as I constantly avoid his lips.

'I have never kissed anyone before. I don't even know how to kiss,' I whisper shyly into his ear.

I am so close to knowing what it feels like to be kissed; I would love to experience it. What am I waiting for? I have already denied myself so much. *But I must stop thinking such crazy things! I cannot kiss this man. I cannot let him take away my self-control as well as my dignity …* But I'm still cuddling him, caressing his face and hair, kissing his neck, his ears. I am lying on his body, feeling so relaxed.

He sends me for another drink. He is getting sleepy now and doesn't even take a sip, barely able to keep his eyes open. There doesn't seem much point in staying. By the time I have dressed and am ready to leave, he is already fast asleep.

On Undefended Flesh

I step outside onto the streets of Chelsea, reflecting on this extraordinary day: the first time ever I have been close to a man. He managed to loosen my self-control, unleash my desires, making me understand what it must feel like to be a woman. In my mind he is no longer a brutal master, but a man with a tender and loving side.

I text him when I get home:

/I wanted to stay with you tonight but you got drunk and fell asleep./

He does not reply, probably fast asleep. In the middle of the night, around two, I wake and check my phone.

/I am sorry you are not here./

6

Falling in Love with my Daddy

/Little girl should report to her Daddy for her next punishment on Thursday 5pm. You will stay overnight, sleeping with your Daddy after you have received the severe beating you deserve./

Staying overnight? Sleeping with him? He does not even ask if I want to or not. It felt incredible cuddling him last time, but should I really be giving up my virginity?

/Little girl is looking forward to the next session. This will be the first time she spends the night with a man./

On Undefended Flesh

He greets me with a big hug and kisses my cheeks. He smells so nice; his face is freshly shaven and so smooth. My arms are around his neck as he holds me tight.

'My little girl,' he whispers gently into my ears.

'My Daddy.' I feel so warm, so secure in my Daddy's embrace. We are standing in the hall, hugging each other for a long while, until he takes me into the dining room.

'Now show me your bottom.'

I know he wants to check whether I have visited any other masters. I pull down my panties confidently: except for some faint marks left over from our last session, my body is pure.

He inspects me thoroughly.

'That's acceptable. Now turn around.'

He is looking at my pussy.

'You should get rid of that hair as soon as possible. You must shave,' he says, looking disappointed. His face turns all serious. 'Get changed and wait for your Daddy here.'

Now I'm quite thrilled to be putting on my uniform. Something exciting will happen when I put it on: pain but also pleasure. My heart beats faster as I hear him approaching. He takes me by the hand to the living room – no more crawling or hair pulling.

We start off with the footstool.

Now he wants me to lick his shoes clean.

'Lick the sole as well.'

Falling in Love with my Daddy

Obviously it's not hygienic, but I cannot say no. I cannot destroy my submissive image and make him disappointed. I must prove to him that I am completely obedient and humble, even if it means licking the sole that meets all the filth.

I run my tongue over it.

'Now go to the kitchen and get me a drink. The same as last time – half, half.'

Oh my God! Shame on me – I cannot remember for the life of me what his drink is made of. I know he will be angry, but I need to ask rather than make some strange cocktail.

'I know you will punish me for it, but I forgot what your drink should include.'

'Yes, Daddy will beat his naughty little girl for forgetting Daddy's favourite drink. Half gin, half tonic, four pieces of ice. Over my knees, you dirty piece of shit.

'... worthless, insolent girl. Now you will always remember how to make Daddy's favourite drink properly.'

I run to the kitchen to fetch his proper drink.

'On the floor, footstool!' he growls on my return.

He continues watching television, but I soon get bored under his feet.

'Can I talk to you?'

'Shut up,' he replies, not in any mood to chat.

My back begins to ache from the weight of his legs, though it is quite some time until he grants me relief.

'Now you can watch TV kneeling by the sofa.'

I'm kneeling by his side, watching as he switches channels constantly, from soap operas to advertisements, comedies to the news.

'Come here,' he says finally, gesturing for me to come to his lap.

My face is in his lap. He lifts his hand; I shiver with cold expecting a slap, but he smiles at me and starts stroking my hair.

'Daddy's naughty little girl. You know Daddy will have to cane you soon, don't you?' His smile turns somehow crooked as he reminds me that the magic cane is on its way.

'I know.'

'Are you looking forward to being cut by your Daddy?'

'I can't wait. Daddy knows how to make me a good girl,' I tell him, trying hard to feign some enthusiasm.

I am lying on top of him, cuddling and caressing him like last time. He begins to unbutton my shirt, wanting to feel my breasts. As I'm so ashamed of them, I try to convince him not to bother.

'They are so tiny. You wouldn't want to see such disgusting things.'

But he remains unfazed, continuing with the unbuttoning until he has his reward.

'Do you call these breasts?' He pinches my nipples, twisting them till they hurt. Though I've always imagined

Falling in Love with my Daddy

what it would be like for a man to touch my breasts, this is not the kind of touch I expected. 'They are pathetic. You can't call them breasts.'

'I know,' I sigh sadly, agreeing.

After a little more cuddling, it becomes time for the bedroom. It is dark outside. He draws the curtains and shuts the windows fully so no one will hear my screams. I get into my usual position on the bed: head down, bottom exposed high and waiting.

In my heart I am hoping he will not be as cruel, now that our relationship has changed; however, I quickly scorn my naïvety as he cuts into my flesh as fiercely as ever. I cannot keep still. I constantly turn to see when and where the next blow will arrive. And as I look back, I always see the same – cold, rigid, emotionless – expression on his face.

A pristine white pillow becomes sullied with all my melting make-up as I bury my head deeper, hoping to escape the excruciating pain. I'm exhausted, yet try and remain strong, not crying out for mercy. Eventually, it becomes so unbearable I find myself repeatedly moaning '*ne, ne, ne*' in my mother tongue.

'Now the final six. Just be a good girl and keep quiet.'

Another six – it will feel more like sixty on my bruised thighs. School memories of running circuits for my dreaded Physical Education class flash before me – I hated them so much. The last six strokes are like the last six circuits: absolute torture, before I collapse completely.

After it is over I continue crying. He comes over to comfort me, but I am reluctant to let him in, overwhelmed with such conflicting emotions. How can I possibly share tender moments with a man who inflicts such pain? ... *But after the torture, Daddy will provide me with the love and affection I so need.*

'Good girl. Daddy is very pleased with his little girl.'

He is holding me very tight. Daddy's cuddles soothe his little girl as he wipes the tears from her eyes. It all seems surreal and unfathomable: one moment he cuts my thighs ruthlessly, without compassion or remorse, and then he will soothe me with his gentle cuddles and kisses which feel so good.

He takes off his trousers and shoes, throwing them on the floor as we go to bed together. I'm lying on top of him as he kisses me, his lips on my mouth. I try and keep my lips shut but I end up giving way to his intrusive tongue. I can feel it moving around in my mouth. I am helpless, not knowing what to do or how I should behave or react.

'I don't know how to kiss,' I say, ashamed.

'Daddy will teach you everything,' he replies tenderly.

I move my tongue around inside his mouth, touching his tongue and teeth, discovering every corner of it. I'm so excited – *my first kiss!* But these emotions I'm

Falling in Love with my Daddy

experiencing right now, are they real? Is this love or lust? Or perhaps some craving for affection? ... I don't know and nor do I care; for once in my life I just enjoy the moment, going with the flow.

He looks at me affectionately. 'You are gorgeous. My gorgeous little girl.'

Gorgeous! I love that word — it's so expressive, so pretty. *It's amazing that he really thinks that about me.* He stares at my bruises and begins to touch himself, caressing me with one hand and masturbating with the other.

'Do you like seeing Daddy masturbate?'

'Yes, I love it.'

'How much do you love your Daddy?'

'I love my Daddy so much I cannot find the proper words to describe it. You are the first man in my life; I gave you my first kiss, my first cuddle.'

'Do you like it when Daddy canes you?'

There is an uneasy silence. Even though I feel something very different, I reluctantly respond with a 'yes', as I know this is what he wants to hear.

'Ah, ah, ah ...' He sighs lasciviously, ejaculating plenty of stuff from his penis.

'Bring Daddy some tissues.'

He wipes his penis and stomach dry and goes to the bathroom. I gaze up at the ceiling ... *my first kiss, my first night with a man* — somehow it does not make me happy. I thought the whole thing would be more romantic. But then again, what did I expect? Staying with a man who beats me black and blue – this cannot be the concept of love that most people are looking for.

Though I feel confused by all the emotions swimming around inside of me, I am resolved to enjoy a night full of tenderness. However, when he gets out of the bathroom, he gives me a goodnight kiss, switches off the light and turns away from me.

I lie there beside him, thighs throbbing, eventually falling asleep in my uniform.

*

When we wake the following morning, he pulls me towards him and holds me tight; *the first morning with my Daddy.*

'Show me your legs.' He gives me my first command of the day.

I kneel into position, exposing my bottom for him. The usual procedure follows: he masturbates, I fetch some tissues, then he asks for more as he has so much sticky stuff.

'Now Daddy will show you how to make proper English breakfast tea. Next time you will have to do it on your own.'

Outside the bedroom is a large mirror, and I stop in front of it to observe my thighs. Shocking red and violet stripes are crisscrossed all over; no wonder they are so sore. Yet, he does not seem fully satisfied:

'I should have been more severe. You are not bruised

Falling in Love with my Daddy

properly.'

I follow him down to the kitchen. He puts the kettle on, opens the cupboard and removes a big wooden tray, on top of which he places two white cups, teaspoons, a small pot for the milk and a larger one for the tea.

'Listen, I'll show you only once. You put one square filter and two round ones into the big pot. Always use the organic milk.'

He opens the fridge (which doesn't smell too good) and pours the milk. After he fills the pot with the hot water, he asks me to carry the tray up to his room.

Daddy drinks his tea with his little girl, watching the morning news on the BBC ... I cannot take my eyes off him. He is my Daddy, the first man in my life. I adore him. He is so intelligent, intriguing, dominant; and he can be so nice and gentle, particularly after a brutal beating ...

'Do you love me?' I ask between two kisses.

'Yes, I do,' he replies warmly.

'Will you always love me?' I fall into his arms, cuddling him passionately.

'You're such a woman,' he says, smiling.

(I do not know whether to take this as a compliment or offence. Yes, I'm a woman, so what? What is he trying to say?)

He goes to bathroom to take a shower and clean his teeth, before coming out naked. Remaining on the bed, I stare at him, watching his every move. I get up when he returns to the bathroom, following him like a little girl who wants to see her daddy getting ready for work in the morning. He's putting some eye drops into his eyes, and some cream on his face.

'I bought this cream in New York last year. It is excellent against wrinkles. It was advertised on TV and I didn't want to believe that it works, but it does,' he says, full of admiration for his anti-ageing cream. ('... *such a woman*! I think to myself.)

The sound of a female voice drifts from downstairs.

'Who's that?' I ask, agitated.

'Just the housekeeper.'

'But what will she think if she sees me?'

'It doesn't matter what she thinks. Before I forget, here is your pocket money.' He hands me a pile of fifty pound notes.

'Little girl's pocket money from her Daddy,' I say and smile. The pocket money that is worth suffering for.

'Let's go. Daddy is running late.'

Quickly I change into my jeans and T-shirt. He goes down to discuss shopping with the housekeeper, while I try to escape, silently, slowly, on the sly like a thief — but she catches me. We exchange a 'hello', with me looking more surprised than her. Perhaps she is used to seeing young girls leaving her employer's home in the morning.

Daddy grabs his leather briefcase. We leave the house and walk down the street; I'm a couple of yards behind him.

Falling in Love with my Daddy

'You didn't say anything about last night.'

There is no reply. He continues walking in front of me, silent.

'Was it amazing for you as well?' I prompt him.

Still no response.

'Why don't you say anything?'

'I will just ignore you,' he finally says, coldly.

'I don't even know your name ... I spent the night with a man I know nothing about.'

'You don't have to know my name.'

We reach the end of the street where he gives me a little kiss on the lips.

'I'll text you,' he says, then walks away.

I make my way to the bus stop. Everyone is fresh, active and energetic, while I'm walking around with my sore thighs, feeling weird, wondering if there is anyone else out there who is leaving their daddy with cuts and bruises. *Who else?* I look at the women passing by, sure they all have a normal life – a partner who loves them, kisses them without caning, cuddles them without causing pain.

My first night with a man. Did it mean as much to him as it did to me? ... I know the answer, but don't want to think about it.

*

We meet again the following Friday. He has called me for an afternoon session between one and six since his kids will be coming over later that evening. The whole week I've been looking forward to seeing him, thinking of nothing else. Something meaningful is developing between us, I can feel it. Wanting to look my best, I have changed my hairstyle from the usual ponytail into a cute plait.

He greets me with a big hug, caressing me for a long time, then searches for my lips and kisses me.

'My little girl,' he says. He seems so gentle and relaxed today. Though I will soon have to suffer, I'm elated to be in his arms.

I change into the uniform before we go upstairs together. On the bed we caress and kiss each other. I'm feeling so high.

'Why am I doing this with you? I don't understand myself,' I tell him between kisses.

'You are just falling in love with your Daddy.'

Falling in love with my Daddy ... It sounds crazy but I concentrate on enjoying this new pleasure – lips and tongues meeting, holding each other tight, twisting our bodies around each other till we can feel each other becoming hot and wet. We are like this for so long that I begin wondering how long I can remain a virgin ... But he spoils the moment, declaring it's now time for my punishment.

His face and voice miraculously transform as he opens the wardrobe to pick out a cane. I lie there silent on the bed, my sad eyes beseeching that he leave the cane today,

Falling in Love with my Daddy

pleading only for affection.

'Get into position.'

I continue to lie there, staring at him.

'Come on, quickly! Get into position. Daddy has to punish his naughty little girl.'

Languidly I get on my hands and knees and expose my bottom. He pulls down my panties and comes to the side of the bed to caress my face.

'Now ask Daddy nicely to cane your naughty bottom.'

I'm silent, still in a dream of cuddles and kisses; I have not yet woken up to my reality.

'*Ask Daddy nicely,*' he continues, any hint of a gentleness evaporated.

'Daddy, cane me please. Beat me severely because I've been a bad girl and deserve your punishment. Cane me, Daddy, please,' I ask, indifferent; no matter how I ask for something I do not want, I will get it anyway.

'How hard shall Daddy beat his insolent, disobedient little girl?' He wants me to beg for the punishment he will soon reward me with.

'You should adjust the level of punishment to my pain threshold. You shouldn't be harder than before. Don't be too brutal, Daddy, please!'

The first stroke catches me on my right thigh; the next, on my left. He keeps alternating, pausing before he locates the next precise target. I'm always looking back to find out when my next dose of pain is arriving;

On Undefended Flesh

sometimes my assumption is wrong and it reaches my flesh earlier than I predict, whereas other times I scream out before the cane has even arrived. I try to keep still but it is very difficult if he insists on caning me so viciously. And though I have some control over my movements, it is almost impossible to control my voice – I cry out simply because I need an outlet to the pain!

'Keep quiet!' he says, annoyed.

What must his neighbours think when they hear my screams? Probably that he is just having wild sex – not viciously caning his 'worthless adopted daughter'. He cultivates the image of a well-mannered, elite member of society, and yet all the while he is living a double life – indulging his wildest perverted fantasies.

'Are you concerned about the neighbours?' I ask between strokes.

'I don't care about them. I just want you to be quiet,' he says, dishing out an extra-hard lash of the cane.

When the beating is over he cuddles and holds my face in his hands.

'Tell me how much you love your Daddy,' his voice full of cruel irony.

He begins kissing me. At first I am reluctant to kiss back; but my need for affection is much stronger than any dignity that I have left, and it isn't long before I am returning his kisses.

'I love you, Daddy, so much,' I say, swallowing the tears that roll down my face.

Falling in Love with my Daddy

'What do you have to say to your Daddy after your punishment?' He looks at me seriously.

'Thank you very much for the punishment. I deserved it so much.'

'Good girl.'

He looks pleased with my gratitude, and we lie back in bed, kissing passionately. He wipes away my tears and treats me so tenderly. I forget everything in his arms, lost completely in a moment that I wish would never end.

'My lovely little girl. You are very pretty with your new hairstyle.'

I smile back at him. *He finds me pretty* – I so needed to hear that. It's as though time has stopped, since I do not hear or see anything, only him. Maybe this is what they sing about in love songs, write about in poems ... But time has not stopped: six o'clock is fast approaching.

'We've only got half an hour,' I let him know sadly.

'That's plenty of time.'

'No, it's not. I'll have to go soon, so hold me in your arms and love me passionately.'

'You're such a woman.' He smiles, pulling me closer to his chest.

'Daddy, I love you so much.'

'I love you too, my darling little girl.'

'You said I could be your live-in slave.'

'You will be. After the renovations have been completed you will get your room, my worthless adopted daughter.'

'And what about your girlfriends?'

'Well, maybe you can replace them all.'

Replacing his girlfriends? It sounds serious. I look at him, all excited.

'But you will have to accept that my children will always be number one. They are more important to me than anything in the world.'

'I don't mind if your kids come first. I'd like to be the second most important thing in your life. I am also your child – your *third* one ... your worthless adopted daughter.'

He smiles and kisses me gently. We head downstairs to the kitchen where he hands me my pocket money.

I turn to him. 'We didn't talk about anything. I wanted to discuss so many things with you.'

'Yes, we need to talk about certain things, where we should go from here. For instance, the money. I won't be able to pay that much every time – it's an awful lot. And the fact that I pay you –'

'I know. We have to clarify so much. Everything has changed – I'm not just your slave. I want to know how you feel. I just need to feel secure.'

'Secure!' He laughs. 'Nothing is certain in life. I'd like another twenty million, then I might feel secure.'

He starts preparing things in the kitchen, taking out bowls, pans, cutlery from the cupboards.

'Are you going to cook?'

'Daddy is going to cook for the kids. I love cooking.'

Falling in Love with my Daddy

'I can't cook at all. I've never tried,' I confess.

'I'll teach you someday.'

I wrap my arms around him. We hug for a few more minutes, till he leads me to the door and I know my time is up. We say goodbye with a kiss. It was such a wonderful afternoon and I feel sad to leave. I would love to be part of his life, his family; I want him so much. Do I want the cane as well, though? Or those markings on my body, which I have to pretend to like and which leave me in terrible pain for days? *Perhaps I will come to like it ... if it makes him happy.* Now I feel so confused.

*

The following day, after work, I text him.

> /You are the first man in my life. You gave me my first kiss, first cuddle. It meant so much to me. What does it mean to you?/

It sounds ridiculous – overblown. How can I be behaving like this?

An hour goes by and still no response. I send him another one.

> /I would like to be with you tonight to kiss you all over, hug you and talk to you. Can I visit you right now? I could be there in half an hour./

On Undefended Flesh

I'm extremely tired, yet ready to run to him at any chance.

> /I'm taking kids out, driving them to a birthday party. Can't meet you now./

I'm crushed ... thought he would be happy if I visited ... and now he refuses me ... the kids?

> /You stirred my emotions. I fell in love with you. I think of you all the time. I can't wait to see you again./

These words are way too strong, but I'm overwhelmed with emotions and cannot control myself. I feel as though I am going mad ... particularly if he does not reply to my texts ...

> /My mind says I should stop with you but my heart says carry on. What shall I do?/

Eventually he responds:

> /Just follow your heart. And be patient. You might be pleased with the outcome./

But I'm not pleased.

Falling in Love with my Daddy

/I just can't wait anymore. No one needs me. I may kill myself soon. I'm so worthless – a piece of shit, like you always say./

It is after midnight and my texts are getting crazy – just like me. And now there are no more replies. *How could I be so stupid as to text something so dramatic? Now I've blown it! I could have had a relationship – my first! But no, I was too impatient, just couldn't wait.*

I sit around for hours, crying, cursing myself. When I do eventually try to go to bed, I fall in and out of mad dreams. I'm feeling so out of control right now, and I'm worried that the outcome will be just like the time my emotions again got the better of me; my mind drifts back to that day, and those subsequent weeks …

They found me strolling down the street, dazed, in my pyjamas. I had just taken a concoction of pills – painkillers, antibiotics, antidepressants – everything that was in our medicine cabinet.

During the previous two weeks I had been behaving hysterically, horribly depressed, unable to stop crying. So many things had gone wrong. My grandmother – who meant everything to me – had passed away unexpectedly. My job was getting worse; I could no longer control my class and the kids had no respect for me. Also my sister (who had always been my best friend) was no longer speaking to me. I was sick of everything – sick of my dysfunctional relationship with my father – sick of living! I wanted to sleep and never wake up.

On Undefended Flesh

I was taken to a psychiatric hospital where I was to spend the next few weeks. Those weeks were to become the most searching of my life.

At first, everything was so peaceful – no news, no hassles, no pressure; everyone and everything seemed slow inside (no doubt, because of the antidepressants and sedatives that were liberally prescribed). I would spend my days listening to people's stories, their tragedies, and how they ended up in here. I even started to question my idea of normal – after all, who is normal? – and whether those people in the 'real world' were any more normal than us.

As the days passed by, however, I began to feel more uncomfortable, particularly when my poor mother would come to visit. She came every day, sitting on my bed with my favourite chocolates, her undivided attention on me ... the attention I secretly craved. But it was not a pleasant feeling – particularly as I could see she was blaming herself for my troubles. I realised the immense burdens she herself was under; already distressed by her mother's death, I had to compound her grief, not to mention the fact that she was trying to hold down a demanding job, look after her ill father, and endure her bitter marriage with an argumentative and jealous husband. I started to worry that she may soon be having her own breakdown.

And then there were those nights: listening to the patients in the casualty department as they became violent and out of control, screaming and fighting with the nurses. Would I end up like that? I became terrified by the prospect of having to remain in a psychiatric hospital indefinitely, being seduced by drugs, losing my free will, my freedom, my future. I was only twenty-three, still young enough to change my life.

My fears were soon realised, however, and the earlier illusion of an ideal retreat quickly transformed into the reality of a veiled prison as the doctors became reluctant to grant my liberty. Hours would slip by as I fantasised my imaginary escape from that psycho-jail. But it was only due to the steadfast insistence of my mother that I was finally granted the doctors' permission to leave.

Two weeks later, I had given up my job and the support structure of my family (which is the only support structure I had ever known), and followed my dream of living in England.

*

The following morning I wake feeling more composed and text him again, asking to meet for a chat.

/I'm at a barbecue with friends. Can't text you all the time. You can come to my place at 9pm for a chat./

When I arrive he greets me with only a hug – no kiss. He looks rigid, not loving and affectionate at all. He directs me to the living room and I sit beside him on the sofa.

'So tell me about your silly texts.'

'I'm so ashamed. I don't know what came over me. I just went crazy.'

'Yes, you did. Especially when you mentioned that

suicide crap,' he says, looking at me seriously.

'I didn't mean it, I just wanted to be with you. My emotions have gotten out of control. After the kissing and cuddling ...' but I cannot finish, and burst out crying.

'Listen. I've got a complicated life. I've got the kids. I have the girlfriends around. I travel a lot. And then you entered my life and suddenly everything happened too quick.'

'You don't want to see me anymore?' I ask, struggling through tears and the possibility of losing him for good.

'I don't know. If it is the only way for you to get rid of these nutty emotions, then I suggest we should say goodbye.'

'But I don't want to lose you.' I cry desperately, waiting for the moment he will take me in his arms and wipe away my tears. But he does not; he just watches the TV from the other end of the sofa. Impulsively, I sit on his lap and wrap my legs around him, kissing him with abandon.

'I came here tonight for the last time ... for my last portion of love,' I whisper to him.

Soon he is kissing me back. He takes out his penis and rubs it.

'Will you cry for your Daddy?' he says, aroused by my tears.

'Yes, I will cry a river for you.'

'Do you like seeing your Daddy's penis?'

'Yes, I do. I love watching my Daddy's nice, long,

Falling in Love with my Daddy

thick cock.'

'Do you like being beaten by your Daddy?'

'Yes. I love it when you ask me to bend over into position, lift up my tiny pleated skirt and pull down my panties ... while I expose my bare bottom on your big bed and you cane me brutally, cutting my pure white thighs deeply, making your worthless adopted daughter suffer in pain. You are the best Daddy in the world. You know how to treat your little girl properly.' I whisper it all into his ear as he continues to rub his penis, savouring my words.

Soon he is asking me for tissues ...

I feel proud of myself, having managed to arouse him with only my presence and words (not having needed to be beaten!). I try and cuddle him, sure that he will be nice to me after his orgasm, but he remains cold.

'It's late now. I think you should go home,' he says.

'But I want to stay a few more minutes.'

'I'm tired and want to go to sleep. Go home. Even if you were the most beautiful girl in the world I would still want you to leave.'

His words pierce my heart. How can he be so heartless, so rude? He has relieved himself, gotten his satisfaction, and now I must go home. Some men might be happy if I stayed with them for the night, but not this one – throws me out like garbage! I feel unwanted and humiliated, and shut the door behind me without saying goodbye.

It is almost midnight on a Sunday night. Hardly any

cars are on the streets. Shops and pubs are closed, no one is about. Strolling down the street, I pass the empty shops and stare into the big glass windows ... they're staring back at the sad, lonely girl.

*

When I get home I slip into bed. *How can I carry on? Why did I let him hurt me? Where have I left my dignity, my self-control?* The respite of sleep will not come to alleviate my desperate feelings. I get up and delete his number from my phone – I want to delete him from my thoughts, my life, my memory! From now on he is dead, does not exist. But as the hours tick by, he is still in my head and it seems impossible to sweep him away. All I have now is his email address ...

> *Dear Daddy,*
> *I want to start all over again with you. I would like to be your proper live-in slave. I will be absolutely humble and obedient, completing all your commands, obeying all the rules you set me.*
> *Your little girl*
> *Shana@*

I'm surprised and delighted when a few hours later he texts me.

/Got your email. Will you really do anything

for me? If you want to be my live-in slave you have to adjust to some very strict rules, eg shaving, which is non-negotiable. Also you would be beaten very severely on a regular basis./

He gives me an appointment for Thursday next week. I visit him late after work. I ring the bell and he opens the door, giving me a hug.

'I thought I would lose you,' I whisper as I fall into his arms. 'So what am I going to be? A little girl or a slave?'

'You'll be my little girl.' He kisses me but his kisses do not seem passionate.

We make our way up to the bedroom. I begin cuddling him, nervously trying to figure out when would be the best time to tell him that tonight he won't be able to pull down my panties.

'Daddy … I'm having my period.'

His face becomes upset and he does not say a word.

'It's not my fault, I'm so sorry. You can still beat me, I'll just have to leave my panties on. You always whip my thighs so it won't make any difference,' I tell him, the words tumbling out of my mouth.

'Get into position,' he says angrily.

I imagine the pain will now be doubled because of my period – and it is; the first stroke gives me an idea how terrible the rest of the session will be.

'Now what do you have to say?' he says.

I hesitate as to what is the correct answer. 'Thank you, Daddy.'

'That is not enough. You will have to count each stroke, then say, "Thank you, Daddy. May I have another one?" Do you understand?'

'Yes, I do,' I moan into the pillow.

'So now we'll start again.'

I look at him. His eyes are fixed on my thighs, aiming for a precise spot.

'One. Thank you, Daddy. May I have another one?'

'Two. Thank you, Daddy. May I have another one?'

'Three. Thank you, Daddy. May I have another one?'

I continue with the same rhythm, the same routine, though my voice is getting weaker and less articulate the longer the beating continues. I make a conscious effort to pronounce all the words clearly, but sometimes the pain – which is making me scream and cry like crazy – blocks my brain, and the words get lost in my mouth.

'Fifteen. Thank – Daddy. May I have another one?'

'Yes you may. But now I'll give you a break.'

I look at him, surprised.

'Daddy is going downstairs to watch TV. You'll stay here reflecting on the punishment you've received, and that which remains. Don't worry, my darling little girl, you'll get so much more when I come back. Now kiss the cane and I'll be back shortly.'

He positions the cane near my mouth and I kiss it,

Falling in Love with my Daddy

feeling disgusted. He leaves me alone, placing the cane on the bed as my only company. I check the time: midnight exactly. Staring at the ceiling my mind becomes occupied with the lyrics of a Bon Jovi song, 'Midnight in Chelsea'. I used to love that song, but never could I have guessed that it would end up so incredibly real ... *Midnight and Chelsea. Love and Torture.*

I sing softly, exploring the room in the dim light. Clothes are strewn over the sofa, plastic bags and newspapers scattered on the floor, a couple of hair dryers on a chest of drawers ... and plenty of photos of his kids; in one, he is sitting in a restaurant with them, smiling, like a nice, caring daddy. What would they think if they saw their daddy now?

I stop my singing when I notice something peculiar in the corner: an unusual statue on top of a small glass table. I get up from the bed to take a closer look. It's a bronze sculpture of a woman in a familiar position: bending over, exposing her bare bottom, exactly as he gets me to do. He must be obsessed with caning to decorate his home with something like that. But is he not embarrassed when his kids come over? Are they not shocked when they discover such an explicit ornament in their daddy's room?

I hear him coming and run back to the bed, getting in exactly the same position as he left me, the cane menacingly beside me. He leans down to my face, gives me a kiss and inspects my body thoroughly.

'Daddy has to cane you again, harder than before. Then we can go to bed.'

'Will you cuddle me afterwards?' I ask imploringly.

'Of course. Daddy will cuddle his little girl all night long, if you take your punishment properly.'

I quickly get into the same position as his statue. He beats me brutally, cutting my already bruised thighs.

'... *Twenty-five. Thank you, Daddy. May I have another one?* How many left? I can't do it any longer. Give me a break, please – it's *too* painful!'

'You'll receive five more, then we're finished.'

The last ones are the most fierce. I try and keep still for the final assault, knowing at least it will soon be all over.

'*Thirty. Thank you, Daddy.*' I do not ask for another.

I'm exhausted and sobbing, but Daddy takes his little girl into his arms, caressing her gently.

'Good girl. You've done very well. Daddy's proud of his little girl,' he says soothingly.

He takes out his penis and starts rubbing it, pulling my hand towards it.

'Touch Daddy's penis.'

'No, I can't touch it. I don't want to,' I scream out, denying him his wish.

'You have to learn to touch Daddy's penis if you want to please him. You need to learn a lot, but Daddy will teach his little girl.'

He rubs his penis while kissing my lips and holding

Falling in Love with my Daddy

me tight to his chest.

'How much do you love your Daddy?'

'I love my Daddy so much I couldn't possibly find the correct words.'

'Daddy will beat his little girl every time.'

'I got some nice marks from my Daddy tonight.'

'Do you like them?'

'Yes, I do. I love the way you bruise my skin. It is so beautiful, I'm so proud of it.'

He rubs his penis faster as I tell him what he wants to hear.

'Daddy will always make sure his little one has enough marks and cuts on her body. I will beat you black and blue every time we meet.'

'I love my Daddy. I adore you so much. I respect you. I love it when you cane me brutally because I know I deserve it. You are such a good and generous Daddy that you reward your little girl with the hardest cane strokes ...'

'Ah, ah, ah. Tissues! ... More, I need more!' He wipes the sticky stuff off his penis and stomach.

'You always need so many tissues.'

'I know,' he says laughing, proud of how much stuff comes out.

He goes to the bathroom while I wait for him on the bed, sure that my portion of love will soon begin. After a few minutes, he returns.

'Daddy's going downstairs to watch TV and have a

cigarette. Then he'll come back to his little girl.'

Disappointed, I hide under the duvet and continue to sing my song from before. He promised me the kisses and gentle touches that I need, but instead just leaves me here. Is every man like that or just him?

Half an hour later he returns.

'You promised to cuddle me all night,' I say angrily.

'Yes, I will. Daddy will cuddle his little one all night long.'

He jumps into bed and we start cuddling.

'What's that statue in the corner? Who's that woman?' I point to the bronze sculpture.

'That's Tracey, my Australian girlfriend.'

'Is she the one who can take one hundred strokes?'

'She is. A friend of mine who is an artist made it for me as a present. She posed for him.'

'It's quite provocative.'

'Yes, it is. I like it.'

'Was she a good girl?'

'Very good. And she was shaven, unlike you.' He looks at me seriously. 'You should shave your pussy – and that's not negotiable.'

It has always been a principle of mine to stay as natural as possible, for that reason I haven't ever wanted to shave my private parts. Besides, if I shaved it once I'd have to do it again and again, and I do not wish for such a trouble. Why is he so obsessed with shaven pussy anyway?

'Why are you so keen on shaven pussy? It is

Falling in Love with my Daddy

unnatural.'

'Most women shave it — it's so much nicer. Hairy pussies are disgusting. There was a survey in the US regarding shaving. Do you know how many American women shave it?'

I shake my head.

'Eighty percent!' he says.

'That can't be true,' I respond in disbelief.

'Well it is true.'

'I don't care. I'm not American, and anyway —'

'You must shave. Otherwise you will lose your Daddy.' He looks at me with a grave face.

'Yes, I will ... eventually,' I say to reassure him. 'But it's not that easy. You've seen my pussy, it's so hairy. And I've never shaved it, I don't even know how.'

'It's very simple. All you need is a razor.'

'What will you do with me if I shave my pussy for you? Will it even make a difference?'

'We'll see. Daddy will teach lots of things to his little girl?'

'Would you like to take my virginity?'

'I would. I'll take it in three different ways. I'll fuck you in your pussy, in your arse, and in your mouth. All three.'

'I can't ...'

'Yes, you *can*. Daddy will teach you everything.'

He switches off the light and we start kissing under the warm duvet, rolling over each other's bodies.

'Actually, you're quite attractive,' he says to me (under the duvet and in the dark!).

'Did you beat the Australian girl harder than me?'

'Yes, she received much harder beatings.'

'I want to be your best girl.'

'You could be, but then you have to obey completely. And you have to learn a lot.'

'Was she a virgin?'

'No,' he says laughing, 'she definitely was not. I guess you have some advantages over her.'

'I don't think you'd find another virgin submissive like me.'

'You'd be surprised.'

'I'm pretty sure there aren't too many around.'

'Actually, I know one. She works as a waitress in a restaurant. She's also Hungarian.'

I look at him incredulously.

'I'm joking.' He laughs, pulling me towards him, cuddling me tight. Soon, however, he gives me my last and most painful command for the day:

'Now let's go to sleep.'

He turns away and it isn't long before he is fast asleep.

*

Next morning I wake up early. I inspect my body in the huge mirror outside his bedroom; my legs are covered in red stripes and severe bruises – violet, pink and brown.

Falling in Love with my Daddy

Though I am quite used to it by now, I can't help feeling shocked. I make my painful way to the toilet and then go back to Daddy, hungry for him to wake up.

He is roused by his alarm clock, then pulls me into his arms.

'Show me your legs.'

I get on my hands and knees to expose my bottom.

'Should have beaten you harder. That's nothing.'

He takes his penis and starts masturbating again. I am in his arms watching his movements. He pulls my hand toward his cock.

'Touch it. Come on. Touch Daddy's penis.'

'I don't want to.'

He looks upset. 'You have to learn to touch Daddy's penis.'

He starts sighing heavily and I escape from his arms, not wanting to be covered in his sticky stuff.

'Why do you always run away when Daddy's coming?' His head turns toward me angrily.

I do not say anything, just wait for him to clean up so I can get back into his arms. He switches on the TV and we watch the morning news together. I kiss his hairless chest, which is wrinkled yet smooth.

'You're not hairy at all,' I say to him, thinking of his words '... such a woman'.

'That's true. It's a bit embarrassing – especially on my legs. But my arms are very hairy. What's missing from my legs is there on my arms.'

I touch his body gently, stroking his chest, neck, face, nipples. He pulls my hand again towards his cock.

'You have to touch Daddy's penis,' he urges me.

'I will touch it one day. But not today. I'm not yet ready for it.'

'Turn round!' He begins spanking me with his hands, over my fresh scars and bruises. Though it's not as painful as a caning, it still hurts, particularly emotionally.

'Go to the kitchen and make some tea. I showed you last time how to do it.'

Walking downstairs, I try to recall how he made his tea; it's been three weeks so I hope I can remember. I enter the kitchen and fill the kettle with water, and then have to search for its switch – even managing to boil water is an achievement for a kitchen-phobe like me. I take out the wooden tray and place two white cups on it, followed by a small pot and a large one. I open the smelly fridge and pour some of his organic milk. Now how many round and square tea bags? I listen to my intuition – one square, two round ... I don't think he would be able to tell the difference anyway. Fetching the tray up to his room, I serve him his hot tea, becoming anxious when he draws the cup to his lips.

'Is it OK?'

'Yes, it's fine. Good girl,' he says, rewarding me with a kiss as I sigh in relief.

'The first morning tea made by your little girl,' I say,

smiling back at him.

We drink our tea and watch TV together. His hand starts shaking when he lifts the cup towards him. Is he old or does he drink too much? I consider his wrinkles, grey hair, fat tummy – why do I even admire him at all?

He finishes his tea and goes into the bathroom to get ready for work. When he has dressed he gives me the usual pocket money and we say goodbye.

'When will you punish me again?' I ask him at the front door.

'In two weeks time. I'm going to Japan next week. The British mobiles don't work from there, so I'll text you when I get back.'

7

New Clients On-Board

Two weeks without my Daddy – I reckon it is a good opportunity to visit other masters that I have been neglecting. Daddy demands exclusivity, but my wounds should have healed by the time he gets back. Yet, why am I even bothering? I have a full-time job and a good bit of money saved up; and besides, these new clients can only pay a fraction of what I have gotten used to. Am I just a 'money-grubbing whore' like Marcus said?

In the back of my mind I realise that this sub world that I have stumbled into remains the only bit of security I really have. I may lose my job or Daddy may get sick of me, but I will always have this little niche to fall back on. So *yes*, maybe I have become a 'money-grubbing whore',

New Clients On-Board

but this is the only ticket that is promising me something and I need to hold on to it. Even more fundamentally though: I've finally found something I'm good at. I can deal with the pain, I'm already obedient, and I *do* feel like a shit – all important ingredients in becoming a good submissive. So why would I not explore this strange world and see where it takes me?

*

It's a Wednesday, my only day off from the store this week. I could be relaxing at home having a lovely light day; instead, I'm busy with my unsavoury little hobby, booking myself out to see not just one, but two clients. Feeling quite dispassionate about the whole thing, I tell myself that I have two tasks which I need to complete in order to make two hundred pounds. My first appointment is with a man whose number I store on my mobile as *Nice Master*, since he sounded nice over the phone.

Nice Master asks me to meet him at Liverpool Street Station. He looks pleased when he sees me and hails a cab, giving the address of a corporal punishment room that he has booked in advance. We do not talk; I just look out the window, trying to enjoy my first experience in a real black cab. Eventually, the embarrassing silence becomes too much.

'It's going to rain,' he says as he points out the window.

'Yes, and I don't have my umbrella with me.'

'It's been quite rainy nowadays.'
'Mmm, that's true,' I respond.
'So how was your day, Shana?'
'It was OK.'
'What were you doing this morning?'
'I was dreaming of the marvellous session we are going to have together,' I say robotically.
'That's good. I'm very glad to hear that,' he says, seemingly unaware of my indifference.

By the time we get out of the cab it is already raining heavily, and we quickly run into a block of flats. We take the lift to the fifth floor; all the while he is staring at me with delight. I can feel his thoughts — *'I will soon see her naked, play with her young body, use her for an hour'*.

A relaxed, easy-going man welcomes us in; he runs the business, letting out his flat to people with a penchant for spanking and other such fantasies. We enter a dimly lit room where I become amazed by the dizzying array of implements and accessories on offer — masks, outfits; all types of paddles, whips and canes; as well as other devices for pleasure and pain, some more innocent looking than others. Long black boots with incredibly high heels hang from the walls, their little white tags indicating their sizes. And, to complement the ambience of the setting, gothic music plays ominously in the background.

My master goes to the kitchen to sort out the fee, while I get changed into the school uniform that I have brought with me. He returns shortly, a bottle of white

New Clients On-Board

wine and a couple of glasses in his hands.

'Come and have a glass of wine with me, before I turn into a strict master.'

'Sorry, I never drink while at work. You can drink, I don't mind.'

I hate wine and am not too keen on alcohol in general. But even if I did like it, it would be a silly idea to drink with him: he is a client, not a friend, and I have no desire to know him. I wish to be only an object that he can use for the hour. No soul exists within me now, it's been switched off for the duration of the session.

He drinks his wine while I sit on the floor, waiting for the session to begin. The music is loud and we have trouble hearing one another. He tries to lower the volume but can't work out how to ... It's becoming more uncomfortable.

'Shana, kneel down in front of me,' he shouts over the music.

I get on my knees obediently. He sits on a chair as I look up at him. He's shorter than me, with grey hair, and not much of it – and old ... old enough to be my grandfather.

'You've been a very naughty girl. You need to receive strict punishment this afternoon. Don't you?'

'Yes I do. I was late for school, cheated my exams, played truant. I deserve a thorough correction.'

'Good. The first thing I'm going to do is a firm hand spanking on your bare bottom. So take off your panties and bend over my knees.'

I still am averse to removing my panties, but unfortunately it is a necessary job requirement. Reluctantly I take them off and bend over his knees.

As he smacks my bottom, the only word that could describe how I feel is numbness. I do not feel anything – an inanimate object in a state of nothingness. I do not even cry out or make a noise. He begins spanking me harder, and only now do I moan to give the impression I am suffering under his strict hands. Then he rubs my beaten bottom; though I do not like it, I do not say anything in case he should take offence. He continues with the rubbing, his sweaty hands stroking my skin as though wanting to pleasure me. I try and remain silent but eventually it is too much.

'I've never been rubbed on my bottom by my previous masters before. They just beat me hard but there is no massage at all,' I tell him, hoping the penny will drop.

'I always do it with my spankees. It speeds the healing process, eases the pain. How does it feel?'

'It feels good, but I don't deserve such a delight.' What would he say if I told him how repulsed I was by his sweaty old hands over my body?

'Shana, you can stand up now. Lift up your skirt and show me your bottom.'

I face the mirror with my skirt lifted, watching him in the background as he inspects my red bottom. I know he will not masturbate – he told me on the phone – and besides, I could never imagine him doing so. He seems like a pleasant, old man wanting to get up to something naughty, away from his elderly wife. I should be friendlier, more enthusiastic, but I can't help finding the session rather awkward and boring.

'I can see your bottom is not red enough. You've been a very cheeky girl. You haven't learned your lesson yet, have you?'

'No, not yet. I need more punishment if I'm ever going to be a good girl.'

'Then what are you waiting for? Come over my knees as I want to give your naughty bottom a firm treat.'

I bend over his knees, trying to give the impression I am enjoying myself even though I'm finding it increasingly more difficult. I make some weak and not too convincing cries as he spanks my bottom. It's obvious he is not interested in hurting me at all, yet I still find it tedious to role play with him. He wants me to enjoy the session, but I don't. He thinks I like it if he massages my bottom after the spanking, but I don't. He's rubbing my skin gently and sensually, and I'm finding it extremely annoying. I try and remain silent, but eventually I snap:

'We agreed that there would be no touching,' I cry out angrily.

His hands stop their motion over my bottom; soon they are off my body completely and an embarrassing silence follows. I get up from his knees and kneel on the floor. He looks upset, but he needs to know that I came here with the intention of working and earning some money, not so I could be pampered by his old hands.

'I didn't touch you at all. I don't know what you are talking about. I like stroking red and sore bottoms, that's all. It's essential for me during the session.'

'But I'm not used to it. I need you to be strict and firm. You don't have to be kind and gentle with me,' I tell him.

'All right. If that's what you want,' he says resentfully. 'Stand up and take off your clothes.'

'Everything?'

'Everything!'

Though I'm still not fond of being naked in front of a stranger, it's far preferable to any form of sensual touching. I shed my clothes. He rests his eyes on me for a moment, before placing me into cuffs that dangle from the ceiling. I'm facing the mirror again, and it is not a pleasant picture that greets me.

'Spread your legs apart. I'm going to strap you now.'

He starts beating me with a strap, hard, though not quite enough to make me cry.

It's a surreal view from the mirror: a naked girl, her hands cuffed and strung up towards the ceiling, an elderly man beating her from behind. She has sad eyes and a miserable face. Why is she here? How has she ended up like this?

I cannot believe that the girl in the mirror is me. She is the antithesis of my old self – provocative, without dignity, doing things for money or in the name of money. She looks so unhappy, aimless, lost. Should I feel sorry for her? Should I sympathise with her?

How long can she keep pretending that this is easy money? That it's good for her to let her hair down and do something out of character? But guilt is more painful than anything physical, and she lets the devil in her mind deceive her ... *I am being used, so therefore I am useful. I have a role in society, something I'm good at. It helps me financially and gives pleasure to men.* And that is the end of the fight for her soul.

When the strapping is over he takes me out of the cuffs.

'Now you'll be caned. Bend over the whipping bench.'

'But you promised that it would not be brutal,' I protest.

'Who said it will be brutal? I wanted it to be playful, but you asked me to be strict.'

He's right of course, it was me who asked him to be strict. I just don't want any markings to be visible by the time I visit my Daddy next week.

'How many cane strokes will I receive?'

'I haven't yet decided.'

'You know you can't be too hard. Not for one hundred pounds.'

'*Excuse me!* I booked a session with you, so I'll decide the level of punishment.'

'Sorry. It's just that I'm going to visit my Chelsea master next week and he wants me with pure bottom and thighs.'

'Don't worry, you won't have any severe marks. I'm not a sadist. You'll get six firm strokes.'

He looks at me with a strict but disappointed face; he is not satisfied with my performance – and neither am I. In a session like this there is no place for negotiation, all the details have been agreed to beforehand by the parties. He told me what to expect and now I'm trying to renege.

'You'll be rewarded with an extra five pounds for every subsequent stroke after the sixth.'

He canes me firmly, though it is still much softer than what I am used to.

'Thank you, Sir. I've had enough,' I inform him after six strokes.

'Are you sure you want to stop? I told you I'd pay extra.'

'Yes, I would definitely like to stop. I don't want to risk any deep markings.'

'Well I had something else in mind when I contacted you about your so-called submissive service,' he says, annoyed.

'I'm awfully sorry. I was a bad girl today, I know, but –'

'No, that's not true. You were a good girl. But I expect you to enjoy the session too, and I don't feel that

New Clients On-Board

you did.'

I'm still lying on the bench, relieved that the session is over but disappointed by my performance.

He puts his hand in his pocket to take out my fee, looking a little upset; when he hands it to me I can tell he thinks it has been a waste of money. After I am dressed we walk to the train station together and say goodbye.

'Next time I will be a better girl,' I promise him.

He gives me a kiss on the cheek and we part.

*

My next appointment is across town, at the Hilton Paddington, where the man is staying. When I get there I wait outside as he requested. There is only a well-groomed guy about, and he puts his mobile to his ear to make a call. My phone rings ... *caller unknown*; could it really be him? After the men I've met in the spanking scene it seems far-fetched that a handsome, young, decent-looking guy could be my master tonight. But he's the only man around, so I walk up to him.

'Hi, I'm Shana. Are you waiting for me?'

'Hello. Nice to meet you.' He smiles at me. He cannot be older than thirty-five – tall, red hair, blue eyes and a friendly face. As we make our way to the lift I notice he also has an accent.

'Where are you from? You don't sound English.'

'I'm from Sweden.'

'*Sweden?*' I look at him in surprise. 'I thought spanking

is an English peculiarity. Even Swedish men like it?'

'Of course we do. You'd be surprised how popular it is there.'

'Are you experienced? – I mean, you look quite young. All my other masters have been older men.'

'Don't worry, I'm quite experienced. I've spanked several girls, including my girlfriends.'

'Have you hired spankee girls like me?'

'Yes. I've met submissive girls from all over the world because I travel a lot. Thai girls, Japanese, American, German ...'

'Why do you travel so much?'

'I work for a telecommunications company. I'm in charge of overseas development, so I'm abroad most of the time. I thought it might be fun to try a London spankee while I'm here.'

He seems like a really friendly and genuine person. We carry on talking as we make our way down the corridor and into his room. Then I put on my uniform in the bathroom. When I reappear, he looks impressed with my outfit.

'You're a very pretty schoolgirl, but you've been very naughty lately so I have to punish you. Am I correct?'

'Yes, you are absolutely correct.' I turn my head to the floor, looking ashamed. Unlike my previous appointment, engaging in this role play feels effortless.

'So tell me how naughty and mischievous you've been.'

New Clients On-Board

'Well ... I was late for school. I also fought with my classmates, talked back to the teacher, and smoked cigarettes outside the school with some other girls.'

'I'm really disappointed in you. How could you be such a bad girl? You know you deserve a severe punishment now, don't you?'

'I certainly do.'

'Come here.'

He is sitting on the bed. I walk up to him.

'Keep standing there. Legs apart. Hands on your head.' He inspects me thoroughly – my legs, skirt, face, my whole body.

'Turn around.'

Now he checks me out from behind.

'Lean down. Touch the carpet.'

I do not like this instruction since I've never been able to touch my toes with my legs straight, but I try to do the best I can.

'Come over my knees.'

I bend over his knees and he pulls down my knickers. He begins spanking me with his hand, all the while he is talking to me, building up the scene.

'Naughty girl. Don't you want to be a good girl?'

'I do. That's my biggest dream – to become a good girl.'

'That's why I need to spank your naughty bottom. Bad girl. You should be ashamed of what you've done. Smoking, fighting, playing truant, not showing respect to your teachers.'

'I do apologise.'

'It's too late for an apology. You need to be spanked thoroughly so you can learn your lesson.'

His hands are firm yet still rather playful. I'm crying out a little; but since we are in a posh hotel, I try to control my voice so as not to cause him any embarrassment.

'Now it's corner time. Stand in the corner for a while. Lift up your skirt and think of your sins.'

I go to the nearest corner and reveal my red and sore bottom.

'You are a very naughty girl. Can you tell me what happens to naughty girls?'

'They are punished severely.'

'Right. Do you think you've had enough punishment?'

'No, I don't think so. I haven't had enough yet. You need to spank me more,' I reply.

'Yes, I must agree with you.'

He motions for me to stand in front of him.

'Take off your clothes.'

'Everything?' I ask, although I know my question will be in vain. (Even in an agreeable session like this one, clothes provide a type of security for me to fall back on — a barrier between me and the client.)

'Yes. Everything,' he replies.

I get undressed, throwing the items of clothing onto

the armchair. I stand there before him, naked.

'You are very pretty. You've got a beautiful figure.'

'I'm not pretty at all. Don't tell me that. Don't flatter me.'

'Yes, you are.'

'I've got such small breasts.'

'Your breasts are really nice,' he says kindly. 'Now come over my knees. I'm going to spank you again because you've been very cheeky.'

My bottom has been in demand today but it's still up for more punishment. Although his hands come down firmly, the whole atmosphere remains light-hearted – in fact, as I lay there across his knees, I realise this is the first session that I could possibly say I have enjoyed.

'I just hope that you'll learn to behave yourself after this hard session. You need to follow the rules or you'll be punished. Am I right?' he says, managing to sound stern yet humorous.

'Yes, you're right. I promise to be a very good girl from now on. You've given me such an impressive lesson on why it is important to respect the rules at all times.'

'Will you be late for school again?'

'No, I won't.'

He gives me a smack. 'Confirm it again, saying "I will always be on time".'

'I will always be on time.'

He smacks me again for good measure.

'Will you talk back to your teachers?'

'I will never dare be rude to them ever again.'

He sends me to the corner again. I stand there facing the wall, sensing his eyes on my red bottom. A few minutes later he announces my redemption.

'You took your punishment very well. Good girl. Come and lie down on the bed. You can relax after the spanking, I'll put some healing cream on your bottom.'

I look at him, surprised — no one has ever bothered with ointments for my sore bottom before. I do not say anything but place my head on the pillow, feeling rather exhausted by two sessions and a trip across town. He's rubbing the cream into my skin with a gentle, slow movement of his hands, producing an unexpected reaction within me: a strange, wistful state. *Where on earth are these tears coming from?* I bury my head deeper into the pillow to keep him from noticing, though there is no burying my memories ...

My mother always maintained that my relationship with my father was normal — but how on earth can that be the case? For how could a child not remember a single conversation with their father — not a single one! There was none of that rapport that I would witness between my classmates and their fathers; no questions about my day at school, or how I was doing whenever I felt sick. He would never even scream or get upset with me. Just nothing!

On top of that, there wasn't any non-verbal communication between us either: no eye contact, or such physical phenomena as

New Clients On-Board

a kiss on the cheek or a hug. We may have lived under the same roof but there was an ocean of distance that separated us.

And the worst part was, I never knew what had gone wrong. Had I done something to upset him? What a relief it was to finally leave home and come to England, for no matter how comfortable the house or how sumptuous the meals, I was never able to feel at ease in those surroundings.

... no more strange silences ... no more lack of affection ... no more untold words ... and no more watching my father's drunken rages against my poor mother ...

He continues to diligently rub the ointment into me; as he does so, I can't help wondering what a great father this man would be – loving, communicative, caring. When he finishes, I go to the bathroom and change. He then pays me and we say our goodbyes. Just before I leave, however, he gives me a big hug; I have never been hugged by men until recently, though I've really come to appreciate it ... never rejecting those comforting, surrounding arms around me ... *they feel so good.*

8

Daddy's Little Girl

/Daddy is back from Japan and is looking forward to caning his little girl next Tuesday 5pm. A little puddle of tears will form on the carpet./

/Sorry, Daddy's little girl will be working Tuesday night. Can we meet on Wednesday?/

/Spaniard invited me to dinner but I think I will cancel her. Be prepared for a brutal beating. Daddy./

I'm extremely excited by the time Wednesday comes

Daddy's Little Girl

round. I've not seen my Daddy in over two weeks and have been missing his cuddles so much. I'm also proud that he has cancelled on the Spaniard. He's realising just how important I am to him. I'm the first person he wants to see after his travels – not her. I'm getting closer to kicking her out.

In the afternoon I receive a new text:

/Girlfriend might be coming over to pick something up. Need to give impression house is empty and don't want her to arrive the same time as you. Call from down the road first, OK./

That sounds like fun. Pretending to his girlfriend he's not at home, all the while I'm in his arms. It will feel so good, my having priority over her. She will ring the bell but won't be allowed in, because Daddy wants to be with his little girl.

Before the session, I pop into Peter Jones to buy a summer-style tunic as he requested last time we met. I've seen some schoolgirls wear them in the street and they look really cute. It's still quite embarrassing when I enter the schoolwear department, but at least this time I don't have a whole shopping list to deal with. I spot some black and white chequered tunics in a corner, and grabbing one of the larger sizes, I head straight for the counter.

On Undefended Flesh

When I reach the bottom of his street, I call him. He comes out, recognises me from a distance, and sends me a text, giving me the all-clear.

I walk on over, entering the big door he has left opened, and then give him a big hug, hanging on his shoulders, kissing and holding him tight.

'Did you miss your Daddy?'

'I missed you so much.'

'Good. Now pull down your panties so I can make sure you haven't seen other masters.'

Maybe it was that magical Swedish ointment, but my bottom is pure, without any markings, despite those secret sessions a week ago.

'That's acceptable. Now turn round.'

I turn, sure he won't be as satisfied.

'That's revolting! How many times do I have to tell you to shave,' he says, looking quite furious.

'But I've never shaved it and don't know how ... and I was having my period. Give me some time, please.'

'You've had enough time.'

'I will do it for you, Daddy.'

'When?'

'By next time.'

He stares at me angrily. 'This is the last time I accept you with your disgusting hairy pussy,' he says.

'Thank you, Daddy,' I respond, and wrap myself in his arms like a grateful and devoted little girl.

'Maybe you should have laser treatment to get rid of

Daddy's Little Girl

that hair for good,' he whispers into my ear. 'Daddy will cover the expense.'

'Yes, perhaps it would be best. Then I would be completely hairless.'

'But you must do the treatment as soon as possible.' He looks at me with a strict face.

'I will. I'll do it for you, Daddy.' I drop a kiss on his lips before changing the subject. 'I've bought a new uniform. I'm not sure if this is what you had in mind, but I hope you like it. It looks really cute.'

'Then go and get changed quickly and surprise your Daddy. I'll be in the living room.'

I rush to the bathroom to put on my uniform. I love that Daddy is so keen on dressing up, as that it one of the things I like most about a session. Again, the uniform fits perfectly — as though it was made just for me. I check the mirror and am very satisfied with how I look, then crawl into the living room quietly, gazing at him as he watches TV. I'm kneeling by the door, waiting for him to notice me ... his face becomes delighted when he does.

'You are very pretty.' He cannot take his eyes off me, mesmerised by my new dress. 'Come here quickly, my darling little girl. You are so pretty.' He opens his arms wide, inviting me to sit in his lap.

I get up from the floor and run to my Daddy. He smiles at me, cuddling and kissing me gently.

'You look gorgeous in your new uniform.'

'Do you like it?'

'Yes, I love it.'

'So how was your trip to Japan?'

'Good. But very exhausting. Though, I did see a lot of Japanese schoolgirls around in uniform.'

'And did you think of your little girl, who was waiting patiently at home?'

'Of course I did.'

He strokes me and is so tender ... if only these moments would never end. But he soon flicks that switch, turning on master mode.

'On the floor! Footstool.'

I get on my hands and knees, and underneath his legs. He carries on watching TV, smoking and drinking. Sometimes he gets me to crawl around on the floor, or to fetch his half-gin half-tonics from the kitchen. I've now been under his legs for more than an hour.

'You should have met your Spanish girlfriend instead of me. It would have been more fun,' I say, feeling neglected.

He takes his feet off me.

'Come here,' he says.

I go and kneel by his side. Without warning, he slaps me on the face ruthlessly.

'I wanted to see you,' he snarls. I begin crying quietly; he was so nice before, but now he's acting like a total bastard. He puts me across his knees and spanks me hard. 'You are a worthless piece of shit. A useless slut.'

After he finishes spanking me, he kicks me back

Daddy's Little Girl

into a footstool, with skirt lifted so he can view my red bottom.

'Now go upstairs and get ready for a brutal caning.'

I make my way to the bedroom and quickly discover a few things waiting for me. Laid out neatly on the bed are three canes, a white towel, my £600 pocket money, and a book entitled *Shaven Beauties*. It is the last item that captures my attention; *an inspiring gift for your hairy girlfriend*, I imagine.

I flick through the photographs of naked women who are, of course, all thoroughly shaven ... somehow they seem artificial, unnatural. The hair is meant to be a sign of reaching womanhood, but a hairless pussy looks only prepubescent. Though, isn't this exactly what he wants: a little girl who is absolutely hairless for her Daddy? She has so little power in the relationship, however, and if she gives up what she can do to her own body, Daddy will think he can do anything to her. *Little girl needs to stay stubborn ... and disobedient.*

I take a quick shower, then get back into my uniform and lie on the bed. He's coming; I can hear his heavy footsteps on the stairs. He enters the room and reaches straight for a cane, testing it first by twisting it.

He proceeds to cane me viciously, making me scream with every stroke. I try and stay strong but cannot fight back my tears.

'Just five more and you'll get your first break.'

After the final stroke, he leans down to my face,

On Undefended Flesh

whispering into my ear: 'What do you have to say?'

'Thank you, Daddy,' I mumble slowly.

He puts on a DVD and takes me into his lap; *my first spanking movie* ... It's in Czech with English subtitles, though there's not much conversation taking place, only violence. A petite blonde woman who is dressed up to look like a little girl is told off by her parents, then her dad beats her black and blue with a cane; she struggles, but is tied down by her father's strong hands.

It is a surreal moment as I see the pain which I had just experienced – felt first on my own skin, then watched as an outsider on someone else's. I watch with interest, shocked by the severity of the beating, feeling a true empathy towards the girl.

I take glances at Daddy to see how he is reacting; he's checking on me also. Sometimes our eyes meet as we try and interpret the emotions that are being triggered within each other. I'm scared and horrified: he seems enthralled yet serious. The girl is crying desperately. In the most bloody scenes I hide in his arms, looking for comfort in his embrace as though it were a horror movie; during the climax of her most brutal beating, he gives me a tender kiss on my cheek.

As soon as the movie has finished, he asks me to get into position for the second part. He is really carried away now, and beats me with all his strength. I cry and scream for mercy, trying to move out of position, but he remains unyielding.

Daddy's Little Girl

'Be a good girl and take your punishment properly ... like the girl on the film.'

'But it hurts so much!'

He grabs my arm and throws me back into position. The pain is that tormenting I am so close to jumping from the bed and running out the room. Instead I lie there, listening to the cane slicing through the air, waiting for it to reach my damaged skin.

'Ten more strokes, then it is over,' he says, trying to encourage me.

I feel so weak and cannot move. My body is drenched in sweat, and the pillows beneath me soaked from tears. I'm so ashamed at what I've become, allowing myself to be tortured like this by a wealthy Englishman. I can feel my grandmother looking down on me right now ... ashamed also.

Finally he announces my last three strokes. I'm too exhausted to scream, just cry quietly. After it's over I get up from the bed and drop to the floor, absolutely weak and powerless. He kicks me several times, causing me to twist and turn on the carpet, then he takes out his penis, aroused. In a couple of minutes I am hearing his heavy sighs ...

He rests on the bed, contented; I rest on the floor, exhausted and spent of energy and dignity. Soon he comes to comfort me but I firmly reject his hugs, turning away from him. Instead I go to the window, wrap myself around the curtain and gaze at the lights outside. How

On Undefended Flesh

can I possibly accept comfort from a man like this? No matter how hard I try I'd never be able to explain it.

The pain that I've just experienced, however, is quickly subsiding. Soon it will be as though it never existed. All that will be left is relief and joy: relief that it is all over, and joy that I will soon receive some comfort from the only man who has been willing to give me some.

It is not long, thereafter, when I find myself back in his arms, and he cuddles and soothes me.

While we're hugging, I notice something strange on the bed.

'What happened?' I ask, pointing to the wooden pieces in disbelief.

'I've broken a cane on you,' he says, smiling. 'I'm so proud of my little girl.' He looks very satisfied.

'I can't believe it. You really broke a cane on me. Has that ever happened before?'

'Yes, once on my Australian girlfriend.'

I'm staring at him, shocked.

'You were a good girl tonight. Daddy is so proud of you.' He pulls me closer to him.

'But how could it break? I didn't hear anything.'

'I'm also surprised. It just broke at the end.'

'So you are happy with your little girl now?' I cuddle him, hoping that the broken cane will bring us together.

'Daddy is very pleased with his girl.'

Daddy's Little Girl

His penis is pushing up against my panties. It is so hard and I'm getting all wet.

'What if Daddy would just slip into his little girl's pussy quickly right now?' he whispers into my ear.

My senses say yes, but my mind is still thinking differently.

'I'm not ready for it. Not yet.'

'I'd like to rape my little girl as soon as possible.'

'Would you like to rape me in my uniform?'

'Yes, either your school uniform or Mickey Mouse pyjamas. Would you like to be raped by your Daddy?'

'I want it more than anything.'

'A well-caned, well-raped little girl, pleasing her Daddy,' he whispers.

'When did you last have sex?' I ask him, curious.

'Last week when I was in Japan. The Australian girlfriend flew over to visit me.'

'Was it good?'

'Yes, very good.'

'Will you be violent when you rape me the first time?'

'Yes, a rape must always be violent.'

'But you know that since I'm a virgin it will hurt a lot.'

'Hopefully it will be very painful. But Daddy will cuddle his little girl afterwards.' He is on top of me, kissing and cuddling me tenderly, his penis still rubbing up against my panties.

On Undefended Flesh

'Did you like the spanking movie?' he asks me.

'I did.'

'What did you like most?'

'When the naughty worthless girl was brutally caned. That was my favourite scene. She deserved it so much.'

He's really aroused by what I'm saying, and I'm enjoying turning him on with what he loves to hear.

'Naughty little girls deserve nothing else but a brutal caning. Don't you agree?' he says.

'Yes, Daddy. They should be caned and raped properly.'

'I want to rape you.'

'Will you be wild when you rape me?'

'Yes, Daddy will rape you brutally. In your pussy, arse, mouth. Senselessly.'

'There will be lots of blood,' I tell him.

'And tears.'

'And sticky stuff.'

'Daddy will rape you soon. But you have to shave first. Will you promise your Daddy you will get rid of those disgusting hairs?'

'I promise. But why is it so important?'

'Because little girls are supposed to have nice, smooth, hairless pussies. And you are a worthless little girl who has to obey her Daddy.'

'I love you, Daddy.'

'You're such a woman,' he says, when I wrap my arms around him.

Daddy's Little Girl

Waking up the following morning, we cuddle and he begins masturbating while viewing my fresh marks and bruises. At one point he grips into my injured flesh, causing me to cry out in agony. When he finishes, I go and make some tea; he goes to the bathroom, spending an enormous amount of time grooming himself. We have breakfast before I leave, and he informs me that it won't be possible to see him for the next couple of weeks because he'll be on holidays with his mother. Though I'm rather surprised since he just got back from Japan, I'm not too upset … just as long as he is not with the Spaniard.

*

Hi Marcus,

I have not heard from you for ages. I just hope you are well. I have done several sessions with my Chelsea master so far. He pays £600 every time, which means I have received thousands from him in the past month. I let him kiss and cuddle me because I need it so much. He is the first man who has cuddled and kissed me.

After the caning sessions I spend the night with him in his bed. Lots of gentle touches after the beating. No sex, only cuddles. It feels so good. This is what I really need. But he is so obsessed with shaved pussy. He wants me to be shaven or else he will refuse me, but I don't know how to get rid of those hairs.

Shana@

On Undefended Flesh

Hello Shana,
I've been away on holidays — had a lovely time. I can also give you kisses and hugs, since you sound like you need it. He must be seriously loaded to give you that much money every time. He will surely want to have sex with you soon. You will need to decide if you want to remain commercial or start a relationship with him. For me, it is always non-commercial and NSA.

I suspect that you are lonely, scared and unsure of yourself. And at your age it is ludicrous that you do not have any sexual experience. Of course, he should fire you if you do not shave, particularly in this weather as you will stink. (HINT: Try Veet + Aloe Vera.) I prefer shaven pussies for licking, spanking and fucking — all delights that a money-loving whore like you denies herself.

It is time for me to cane you as you are such a disaster.
Marcus@

I decide that I will have a couple of sessions with other masters while Daddy is away. I make arrangements to meet a man called Andrew next Wednesday. Hopefully this will give my body enough time to heal, though he said over the phone that he did not mind if my body was still striped when he sees me.

The next few days go by slowly, just going to work, feeling bored. I'm missing my Daddy and am so pleased

Daddy's Little Girl

when he texts me, even if the subject matter is not that pleasing.

> **/Are you looking forward to showing your Daddy your nice smooth little pussy?/**

> **/You know that little girl loves you and lets you beat her in every way. But I can't shave my pussy. Why can't you accept me the way I am?/**

> **/If a razor is too much to ask, then Bye./**

I'm petrified now. I do not want to lose him.

> **/I would like to satisfy you completely. Hopefully you are not bored with little girl./**

> **/Daddy is far from bored. You know how to satisfy your Daddy. It's simple: hairless and you have Daddy, hairy and you do not./**

> **/I will have to do it if I will lose you, but cannot understand why it is so essential?/**

> **/Come on. You know shaven pussy is the most important thing. Daddy will be able to watch his little girl's pussy juices drip out after**

> a nice caning. He may even cane the little smooth pussy and watch the blood of the rape mix with the blood of her whipping./

Despite being used to his perverted fantasies, I'm left quite shocked when I read this. Surely he would never really be able to do such things?

> /I don't want to give away my virginity for just one night. Only if you are going to rape me on a regular basis./

> /Daddy will molest regularly. Shave now! Speak to laser people and get price. If OK Daddy will pay. Little girl must be pure and hairless one way or the other when she sees Daddy next./

Wednesday morning I'm on a train to Beckenham with my uniform packed in my bag. Andrew's there in his red sports car, waiting for me at the station. Though he mentioned he was thirty-eight, I did not expect him to look so young ... or to be so friendly and talkative. We chat the whole way back to his house – he about his job in finance, and I about my Chelsea master.

When we arrive I go and get changed, reappearing in the living room in my school uniform a short time later. He's sitting on an armchair, and soon I'm hearing

Daddy's Little Girl

a familiar request.

'Take off your panties.'

I shed my panties and lift up my skirt, revealing my bare bottom.

'He must be very cruel,' he says when he sees the cane marks on my skin. The deepest cuts have not yet disappeared; hopefully there won't be any scarring.

'Yes, he is,' I respond frankly.

'You must have been a very naughty girl if you were given such a severe punishment.'

'Yes, I've been a bad girl. But that's why I'm here. To get punished by you, to become a good girl.'

'Turn around.'

I turn towards him, standing in the middle of the room.

'Legs apart. Put your hands on your head,' he says, his voice becoming stricter.

He inspects me thoroughly, from head to toe.

'So why have you come to my place today, Shana?'

'Because I've been bad and I'm clearly overdue a severe beating. And I know you'll give me what I need.'

'I will indeed. You won't be disappointed. Lie down facing the floor.'

He begins beating me with a belt, which hurts but is bearable. Then he asks me to bend over his knees for a 'sound bare bottom spanking'. Gone is his friendly chatting, he's too busy concentrating on spanking me properly. Next, he gets me to bend over an armchair.

I know I'm in a role play and am getting paid to act, but it's hard to summon any enthusiasm when the cane makes its appearance.

'I love the cane so much,' I say.

He smiles, no doubt aware from my tone of voice what my true feelings are towards this implement. He begins to cane me firmly, though compared to the severe strokes of my Chelsea master it feels rather light. After each stroke I express my gratitude with the usual polite phrase, 'Thank you, Sir. May I have another one?'

After only a few cane strokes, he orders me to stand facing the shelves packed with hundreds of CDs while he goes to the kitchen for a glass of water. If he knew how important music was to me, I'm sure he would move me to the other side of the room; instead I get to stand there like I've just been rewarded, browsing happily through his extensive collection.

'Crawl to the bathroom and put on your other uniform,' he says, when he returns a few minutes later.

I crawl back on my hands and knees, wearing my chequered tunic outfit. He wants me to get into a new bending position, and it's my most humiliating one yet. I'm lying on the floor with my legs bent back over my face and body – my entire genitalia now on display. Though I still have my uniform and white socks on, I feel completely naked, as if even my soul were naked too. He inspects my female organs from a perfect vantage. I feel so ashamed ... the silence only intensifying my

Daddy's Little Girl

embarrassment, compelling me to speak.

'You've got plenty of CDs.'

'I have,' he says, bursting out in laughter.

'Why are you laughing?'

'It's funny that you mention the CDs. They're so irrelevant right now.'

He begins caning my thighs and bottom. It hurts, particularly when he whips the inner part of my thighs, which is more painful. Yet if I compare it to what I am used to, I may as well describe it as humane and soft. The intensity of his whipping increases, however, when he realises that I handle the pain quite well; one of his strokes even lands on my genitals – and not by mistake.

'You can't touch that area. You can beat me anywhere else but there,' I cry out in tears.

'Are you OK?' he says, looking ashamed and genuinely remorseful.

'I'm all right, but you shouldn't have hit me there,' I reply, some anger in my voice.

He starts caning me again, careful now to avoid that part of my body, while I continue to sob. Then he asks me to stand by the wall with my skirt lifted so he can view my markings.

For the final part of my punishment I have to get into another bizarre position: bending over an armchair, my head on the seat, my legs vertical and dangling in the air. He proceeds to cane me again. When it's finally over I am so relieved – not so much because of the caning,

On Undefended Flesh

but because holding that position was becoming unbearable.

'You've done very well. Good girl! You took your punishment properly,' he says, giving me a hug.

His praising words are more rewarding than the £150 he pays me. It boosts my self-esteem in knowing that I can do something well, knowing that I have pleased someone.

We relax and he gives me a tour of his house, showing me his lovely fat cats and some photos on his computer of spanking parties he has attended. There are lots of women about in their twenties and thirties, dressed in school uniform, laughing, embracing and having a good time. No tears, bruised bodies or brutal beatings – only confident women who are not at all submissive, enjoying some fun and games.

He drives me back to the station, imparting some friendly advice before I leave:

'Take care, Shana, and be careful with the mad man.'

*

On the train ride home, I get a text from my 'mad man'.

/**Laser treatment: Harley Medical Group. For free consultation, call _____**/

Daddy's Little Girl

He's mad about shaven pussy. Though I am reluctant, I know I will not be able to hold out for much longer. *Daddy will win and I will be shaven.*

The rest of the day is spent at home in my tiny room, doing nothing except sending text messages to my Daddy.

/Little girl is missing you. When will you have more time for your loving little girl?/

/Daddy will always be busy but should have more time after summer holidays. Would you show your stocking tops off in public after a brutal caning?/

/Little girl wants to grow up and you promised to teach me many things. I would like to be with you at least once or twice a week./

/You will be fucked once or twice a week when I am not away. Sometimes you will come with me. Why do you never answer the points in my texts?/

/Yes, I will show off the marvellous shocking marks on my thighs in public with pleasure. You will be proud as we walk down King's

On Undefended Flesh

Road, you behind me, mesmerised by the sight of my stocking tops./

*

A few more days go by and Daddy is still on holiday in Cornwall with his mum. I make arrangements to visit a new client who lives in Surbiton. He's asked for a morning appointment, since his wife will be at work.

He picks me up at the station – an elderly, sixty-year-old gentleman, like he said on the phone. While driving to his place he tells me about Vanessa, an English girl who used to be his spankee.

'It all went wrong when I got emotionally involved,' he says, reminding me of my Chelsea affair. 'She went mad, but I can't be angry with her. I wanted to look after her. And now she is chasing me. She demands more and more money.'

'Why do you give it to her?' I ask him.

'She's blackmailing me, threatening to take me to court because I beat her.'

'But it was by mutual agreement, wasn't it?'

'It was. But it's not that simple. Even if there was negotiation and consent, I could still be found guilty in court because British laws are very strict regarding violent acts. There is no such thing as mutual agreement if it is about beating and hurting someone physically.'

'Really?' I say, surprised … perhaps this is a bit of knowledge worth filing away. But I know I'm only

Daddy's Little Girl

fantasising and could never really do such a thing; I agreed to get beaten, and therefore, in the end, I can only blame myself.

'I supported her financially by helping her pay out her overdraft, and now I'm getting into debt myself.'

'That's terrible. She's forcing you to pay all her debts?' As I look into his kind face, I can't help feel a tinge of contempt. How could he be so foolish?

'First she didn't force me at all. I just wanted to help her because I felt sorry for her. She suffers from a mental disorder; she has schizophrenia and heart problems. She was abused by her stepfather ... I just wanted to help Vanessa. And now she is blackmailing me, demanding money.'

'Is that why you said on the phone you can't afford to retire from your solicitor's job?'

'It is.'

'Does your wife know about her?'

'She does.'

'And she still lives with you?' I ask, astonished.

He pulls a sad face. 'We live together for financial reasons and convenience. We're not a real couple. We're married, but emotionally separated.'

'But doesn't she notice all this money disappearing?'

'Yes. We've had lots of arguments, but she couldn't stop me.'

Presently we arrive at his home: a modest, detached house in the suburbs, with a big *For Sale* sign sitting conspicuously in the front garden.

'You are selling your property?' I ask, as we enter the front door.

'I have to. I've accumulated so much debt that I can't afford to live here anymore. We have to move into something smaller.'

When I hear this I become worried. Have I wasted my time today, travelling to the outskirts of London to meet a client in such financial difficulty? How on earth can he afford to pay me? Though I am moved by his story, I don't fancy getting beaten for free.

'So you've no money and you've booked a spankee?'

'Ah ... that hundred pounds doesn't matter. It wouldn't help me anyway,' he says, shrugging his shoulders.

I decide to take his word, and make my way to the bathroom to get changed. He then calls me to the living room, where I spend a little time studying the photos on display everywhere.

'Is that your wife?' I ask, pointing to a large photo on top of the TV.

'It is. She's —'

The phone rings. He glares down at it with an agitated expression.

'Why don't you answer it?'

'It might be someone I owe money. They ring several times a day but I can't pay them. I have to pretend I'm not home.'

Now I've heard everything! I want to get straight into the session in case it all turns out to be a waste of time.

'I'm ready now,' I announce.

He puts on a spanking movie and gets me to bend over his knees, proceeding to spank me with his hands. He's a small, skinny man; I can feel his bones while lying on his lap – probably starving because of that girl. He spanks my bottom while watching the video, which also depicts a similar scene. The movie isn't a hard-core eastern European production, but light-hearted English, in which some women in school uniforms get caned on their bottoms until they turn red. I actually nod off in his lap as he continues to spank me so softly, waking only when he asks me to change position.

He gets me to bend over an armchair without my panties. The phone rings again but he does not stop to acknowledge it; instead he proceeds to whip me with a thin cane. Again, it feels so light; he does not wish to hurt me in any way – what a different story it is when I'm in Chelsea. He then asks me to take off my clothes, and he inspects my naked body with interest. I feel obligated to apologise about my breasts when he brings me over his knees for the next part of my punishment:

'I am awfully sorry concerning my breasts. I know they are extremely small.'

'My wife has even smaller ones,' he says matter-of-factly.

I look up in surprise and glance at her photo, trying to make out her figure from under her clothes ...

On Undefended Flesh

Imagine having smaller breasts than me! ... but I awake from my meditation when he enforces the so-called 'Slipper Punishment' on my bare bottom. Who would think that something as innocuous as a slipper could transform into an instrument of pain. Now I'm moaning a little as the pain level increases. He spanks me for a bit before letting me stand up, probably thinking I've had enough.

'You are a good girl. Very good!' he praises.

We're interrupted by the sound of his doorbell, which causes him to anxiously gesture for me to be quiet. What a strange life this man must lead: fearful of a phone call, the chime on his door, or perhaps a car pulling up outside his house. A few minutes of silence passes before he tiptoes to the window to make sure the caller has left. The coast is clear – for now! He sits down, relieved, and we spend some time chatting.

'You've never felt guilty about your sessions with spankee girls while being married?'

'Well, that's always been a question in my mind – whether this is cheating or not? It's not like we had sex, but I'm still perfectly satisfied.'

'So you never have sex with the girls you spank?'

'No, never. That's why I don't really consider it as cheating.'

'Why don't you spank your wife? Won't she let you?'

'I don't know. I've never asked her, but I guess she's not into it.'

'How do you know if you've never asked?'

'I just know her,' he says, disappointed.

'Well, I still think it is cheating even if there is no sex. I'd be very upset if I found out that my partner spanks girls. That's why I feel guilty when I visit clients who are married.'

'But my marriage is literally over. We live in the same place but we have nothing to do with each other.'

There is a pause in the conversation before I continue. 'You seem like a nice person ... you shouldn't let Vanessa manipulate and terrorise you. She's destroying your life, yet you still feel sorry for her.'

'But she is ill ... she really needs help.'

'All I can say is I think you deserve more than this fearful life.'

He sits there looking sad and pensive. When I check my watch, I realise I've been here for well over an hour.

'I've really got to go now.'

'Sure. It was great. You were excellent.'

I smile, hoping his compliment will soon be followed by a financial reward. I'm relieved to see some twenty pound notes in his hand when he returns from the kitchen.

He gives me a big hug at the front door.

'I really hope we can meet again,' he says as we part.

*

On the train I count the notes ... one hundred is not

six hundred, but it was such an easy, pleasant session. There's also a new text message.

> /Daddy's holiday finishes soon, but he has to go straight to the US for a couple of days on business. Daddy wants to see his girl on Tuesday 1st August. Might be able to take the whole day off, certainly the afternoon. We can buy canes, lingerie, skirt and maybe some little girl clothes./

I text him back immediately:

> /Little girl is very excited re next session. What sort of outfit does my strict Daddy require?/

> /I'll give it some thought on the beach and text later./

Ah, he's lying on a beach with his mum ... *I wish I could be there too.*

> /Little girl would like to be with Daddy right now, showing off her fascinating marks and bruises in public so Daddy would be proud of his little one./

Daddy's Little Girl

>/Daddy would buy you an ice cream for being a good girl and asking for a belt whipping later that night./

I smile, imagining myself as a real little girl at the beach, getting an ice cream from her daddy for being good.

>/I would really love that ice cream and the belt whipping too. I love my Daddy. I can't wait to see you again. Send me another tender text please, to make my day./

>/You will become my toilet slave. I will use you to piss on and lick my arse clean. You will be a doormat and I will wipe my feet on your naked body. You will be my ashtray and be tied in chains at the foot of my bed. You will be brutally fisted and raped in the arse./

I become upset when I read this. *'Toilet slave'? 'Fisted'?* Is this what he calls tender? Sometimes he can be so sick.

>/Little girl doesn't want to be tortured all the time. She thought she would be able to have tender moments with Daddy – not tears and pain all the time.

>/Daddy will have many tender moments.

On Undefended Flesh

Sometimes no torture. Just a bedtime spanking, bedtime story, kisses and cuddles, while you play with Daddy's penis down in the country cottage./

That's better. I would like to be feeling those kisses and cuddles right now ...

9

Torn

The following morning I receive a text from my master in Surbiton, which lifts my spirits.

> /Shana, thanks for a really great time yesterday. You are definitely one of the best. Despite how you may feel towards yourself, you are a very nice lady. When we meet next I'll convince you of this, even if I have to punish you until it sinks in. Have a nice day./

A few hours later, as I'm sitting on the bus making my way to work, I receive an entirely different type of text.

On Undefended Flesh

> /I'm not going to have a chance to go cane shopping with you. Can you go and get one? Daddy intends to further his little girl's development by breaking two in one session./

Does he actually intend on becoming more brutal? I need to lay down some limits.

And now another one:

> /You are nothing but a worthless girl. You are not fit for me to shit on. You will suffer pain and humiliation. I will destroy your confidence and own you./

> /You don't have to destroy my confidence AS IT IS ALREADY DESTROYED. You've got very brutal ideas, which makes your little girl very scared./

After my shift has finished, I notice his new text.

> /Go to www._____ and order two DVDs: 'Special Treatment' and 'In the Name of Love', to be sent to your address. Daddy will reimburse you./

Intriguing titles, but why does he want me to order them? Is he too embarrassed to receive the packages himself? I text him asking why.

> /Can't order to mine. Too many inquisitive
> kids. They come in plain envelopes./

Plain envelopes? The whole thing sounds dodgy.

When I arrive home I check the website. There is a vast amount of movies to choose from ... and many pictures of bloody scenes and suffering faces. Remembering how brutal the last movie was that I saw with him, and what Surbiton Master said regarding English laws – perhaps he does not want anything traced back to him. Important Daddy needs to be careful and let his worthless adopted daughter take the blame ...

New text from Daddy:

> /Mistress appointment made for Tuesday
> 9.30pm. Daddy will do most of the caning but
> the mistress will also give you some cuts. You
> will be dressed as a worthless little maid who
> is in training for her first job after school.
> Daddy will tell mistress about naughty texts.
> She'll be very angry/

A mistress? I don't want to be tortured by the two of them. It will be too painful ... and it is much more intimate if it is just me and my Daddy. He doesn't even ask; but why should he, I guess, I do not have any say.

On Undefended Flesh

/How severe will beating be? I don't want to be beaten by a woman. Only Daddy knows how to punish me properly./

/You will be caned until blood runs down your legs. Make sure you are thoroughly shaven./

Now the shaving. Why can't he stop nagging me?

*

Finally, it's Tuesday 1st August. It seems so long since we've seen each other. I am overjoyed that we will soon be spending a whole afternoon and evening together.

/Daddy's at airport. Thinks his little girl would like to see some spanking books at Coffee and Kink, Convent Garden. Meet outside station at 3:30. Bring uniform to change into later, Reform School appointment confirmed. Hope Daddy's little girl understands why a severe whipping is needed./

I make every effort to look pretty for him, since we are meeting in a public place and I want him to be proud of me. However, my choice of clothing – black blouse with spots, black patterned stockings, school miniskirt, scarlet lipstick — may be too bold for someone like me, and I receive many stares from men on the tube and outside the station. There are so many people about, and I begin to feel self-conscious as I stand around and wait.

/Daddy is running 10mins late./

Great! Now I'll have to spend another ten minutes being stared at by passers-by. I hate waiting and cannot tolerate standing in the same place for too long, so I walk up and down the street, stealing anxious glances of my appearance in the shop windows as I pass.

/Where are you?/

Eventually we find each other.

'Why were you hiding down here? I was waiting for you at the station,' he says, annoyed.

'There were too many people. It's more discreet here. I'm so sorry.'

'Well, I think I'll have to punish you for it.'

'I know you will,' I say, giving him a big hug.

'Now let's go to Coffee and Kink.'

'Do we have to go there? You must be tired after your big trip. Why don't we just go home and relax.'

He agrees without too much hesitation. I'm relieved, as I'm feeling self-conscious in these clothes and would be too embarrassed to peruse around an erotic

On Undefended Flesh

shop anyway.

He hails a cab, and we sit together in silence in the back seat.

'You look nervous,' I say eventually, wanting him to speak.

'No, just exhausted from the flight. You're the one that looks nervous. Just relax,' he says, softly stroking my hand.

'I'm worried about tonight. It will be so painful.'

'It will be OK,' he reassures me.

The cab driver seems to be curious; our eyes keep meeting in his rear-view mirror. Perhaps he thinks I'm a prostitute – a young girl in a sexy outfit, holding hands with a middle-aged man. If only I could tap on his little window and tell him I'm not. But why does he keep staring at us, astonished? Doesn't he see young women in the company of older men all the time? So why does he have that weird expression? Do we look like such an unusual couple? ... I try to ignore him.

Aside from the driver's strange glances, I am enjoying my first cab ride with my Daddy; it's so romantic. He smiles at me, stroking my thighs gently, acting all tender. He tells the driver to let us out now, in Sloane Square, outside the massive department store.

'Why did we get out here?' I ask, as we step onto the pavement.

'I thought we could go to the store and buy some accessories.'

'Do you really want to? You look so tired. Why don't we go home instead.'

He seems pleased with my suggestion. I just want to cuddle up with him in his big bed. We walk along King's Road, side by side.

Finally we arrive at his place and behind closed doors. I cannot wait any longer and fall straight into his arms. We're cuddling and kissing in the hall.

'I really missed you,' I tell him.

'My lovely little girl.' He strokes my face tenderly.

We keep on hugging until we realise there are some tradesmen in the house. I quickly run upstairs to the bedroom, while he speaks to them, giving instructions on the work to be carried out. It isn't long before I hear his footsteps on the stairs, then he walks into the room, draws the curtains and gently pushes me onto the bed. There are lots of kisses and cuddles for the afternoon.

'My gorgeous little girl.' He looks at me, smiling, moving strands of hair from my face.

'It's exciting that the builders will be wondering what is going on upstairs.'

'You find it exciting?' he asks, surprised.

'I do,' I reply, hugging him tight.

'You'll be my worthless adopted daughter, no question.'

'And what if I should happen to find a boyfriend?'

'It can't happen. You are not allowed to have boyfriends. And besides, you'll be beaten so severely no man

On Undefended Flesh

will be interested in your bruised body.' His words wipe the smile off my face, and he continues with his twisted fantasies:

'Eventually I would like to brand you.'

'Brand?' I repeat the word slowly, trying to comprehend what he means. 'You want to burn a number into my skin?'

'Yes, something like that. And then you'll definitely belong to your Daddy.' He pulls me towards him, looking delighted by his idea. 'You'll be my branded little girl,' he says, gazing into my eyes lovingly. 'I'd like you to go for a makeover too: nice make-up, sexy clothes, corset, hold-ups. Maybe we should pop into Agent Provocateur. You can also steal Mummy's high heels.'

'How about my hair? Shall I have it cut?'

'No you mustn't. Little girls must have long hair. You should wear them in bunches.'

'And what about my pathetic breasts. Shall I undergo a breast augmentation?'

'You can keep your little undeveloped breasts,' he says, laughing.

'Can we carry on with this bizarre relationship without sex?' I ask, kissing his chest.

'No, we can't. You will have to put a pink ribbon in your hair, and that will be the sign for Daddy that you are ready to be raped.'

'Pink ribbon ... that's so cute.' I move into his arms, kissing his nipples, stroking his face.

'Daddy will rape you in your Mickey Mouse pyjamas, with the pink ribbon in your hair. Daddy wants to break in his girl completely.'

'Will it be painful?'

'Very. Lots of blood and tears. But it will make your Daddy happy.'

The whole afternoon is spent cuddling and kissing. The tradesmen have already left and it's getting dark. I've immensely enjoyed the time spent in my Daddy's arms; however, it's fast approaching 9.30pm, and it upsets me that all these tender moments will have to be followed by a brutal torture.

He turns to me with a serious face, warning me of my appointment.

'It's time to get changed into your uniform. Show me your pussy.'

I look at him, scared. 'But I don't want to,' I mumble hesitantly.

'Pull your panties down and show me your nicely shaved pussy.' He is not smiling anymore.

'I – I haven't shaved it,' I admit reluctantly.

'Go to the bathroom, take a razor and shave it now,' his tone making it clear that this is not a request but a definite command.

'I can't. I don't know how. Let me stay hairy.' I cuddle him, begging him with my gentle touches.

'You know this is not negotiable. I've told you several times. You have to do it. Now!' He is merciless.

'But –'

'NOW!!' His look is so fierce I run straight into the bathroom obediently.

I have lost the game; he has won ... convincing me to do something against my will. But I love him and want him to be happy. Perhaps it's a necessary step in our relationship? Sighing, I begin to shave, careful not to cut myself. Yet I can't help feeling ashamed and disappointed – losing my free will, allowing my fantasy role of being a submissive spill over into real life.

I look in the mirror. It's not immaculate since I did not shave the most sensitive bits, but it certainly looks different – like a little girl. I put on my panties feeling something is missing, and go to show Daddy.

'I know it's not perfect, but that's all I could do.' I anxiously lift up my skirt and he gives it a thorough inspection.

'Not perfect. But much better,' he states gruffly. There is no sweeping joy, no reward cuddle for being a good girl, not even an encouraging smile.

'Get changed into your uniform, we're going in ten minutes.'

*

Now he is the polar opposite of the loving, caring man. Master mode is on: he does not smile, does not speak, does not even let me walk beside him on the pavement.

'Behind me!' He points me to my place. I stoop my

head, feeling inferior, and walk after him. In the cab we sit on opposite sides of the seat; he's checking his notepad, while I'm staring out the window with a sense of foreboding.

We arrive at a beautiful, old building somewhere in Holland Park, and go to the basement flat. A lady opens the door, greeting us with a smile. She looks young, blonde and slim (not what I expected), and is wearing a white shirt, black miniskirt and stockings. She takes us into a specially furnished room which has a similar layout to the place that Nice Master had disciplined me in. There are canes and other implements on the walls, a whipping bench in the middle, and a spooky Vangelis melody playing in the background.

'I've brought her here because she requires severe punishment.' He turns to her, and I get down on my knees without request.

She comes to me and strokes my hair softly. I lift my head to look at her.

'So you've been a bad girl.'

'Very bad,' I reply meekly.

'Get on the whipping bench.'

I quickly climb up. She pulls down my panties and strokes my bare bottom.

'Mmm ... so soft, so pure, such a lovely bottom. What a shame it must be beaten.'

'Yes, and cut,' my Chelsea Daddy adds.

'I will go outside to discuss your naughty behaviour

with your Daddy. We'll leave you here to contemplate your misbehaviour.' Before leaving she whispers into my ear: 'Be prepared for a very severe punishment.'

They are away for quite some time. I just lie there on the bench, becoming bored, listening to that same Vangelis track over and over. When they finally return, Daddy heads straight for the wall and chooses a white cane to beat me with. The first lash is very hard and I scream out in pain.

'What do you have to say?' He is expecting my complete obedience.

'Thank you, Daddy. May I have another one?'

Each stroke is delivered without mercy. I cry and suffer in great pain but do not say anything, not even asking for a break; I want him to be proud of me, and for some reason, I want to impress the mistress as well.

'The last three cuts will be done by her,' he announces.

She comes over to the bench. I'm looking at her with my sad eyes, imploring her to be compassionate. She draws back the cane and hits me with it, but thankfully nowhere near as hard as Daddy. After another two strokes, she inserts the cane into my mouth and leaves the room with Daddy. I feel sickened by the idea of it in my mouth, so I remove the cane with my hands ... but quickly replace it when I hear them returning.

'We have discussed your insolent behaviour outside and reached the conclusion you need much more punishment. We will need to cane you again,' she says. 'I assure you, you will not be bored in the next few minutes,' she adds.

The second round of my 'Reform School' punishment commences with Daddy again, who hits me with all his strength. He cuts my thighs as deeply as he can, not bothering to show restraint in the presence of a stranger; the bench quickly becomes soaked with my tears. When he's finished, I receive the mistress's portion. She whips me lightly, struggling to find any part of my skin not yet cut.

They leave me alone in pain and tears, again with the cane inserted between my teeth. There is not much respite, however; it isn't long before she returns and asks me to crawl outside.

They are sitting at the table; I am on my hands and knees, looking at the floor. Daddy begins to kick into my arse.

'Worthless piece of shit,' he says, resting his feet on me.

'Not fit to be your footstool,' I state miserably.

'Not fit to be my footstool,' he confirms, though still happy to keep his feet on me. 'Useless slut.'

'A dirty piece of shit.'

'You don't deserve to be here.'

'No, I don't.'

'You shouldn't have been born to this planet.'

'No, I shouldn't have,' I reply.

She watches us, laughing, immensely enjoying our screwed-up conversation. After she puts some ice on my bottom, Daddy orders me back to the room, kicking me cruelly in the stomach before I leave.

'She's so cute,' I hear her say, as I crawl away.

Soon they come for me. He chooses the biggest, thickest cane from the wall and shows it to me. I cannot believe that he really intends to use something like that – but he does. He starts hacking into me; I'm roaring like a wolf, making disturbing primal noises, screaming like mad, crying desperately – but he does not stop. I look at her; she looks terrified at what she sees, but does not say anything.

'Six more,' he says. Those six really send me crazy ... screaming in pain ... suffering from his cruelty ... When he has finished he comes to the front of the bench and begins touching my hair, stroking my face, comforting me.

'Daddy is here with you.'

I sob wretchedly. He hugs me, wrapping his arms around me while the mistress gives me the final lashes. She does not use the thick cane but takes a much smaller one, proceeding to beat me gently while Daddy encourages me with soft kisses. When it's finished, they leave me there.

Later, they return to inspect my markings.

'It's not that bad. Quite nice,' she says, touching my skin.

They ask me to stand in the corner. They're close behind me, laughing and whispering; but every time I turn round to find out what they're doing, he slaps me on the face. At one point he beats my head, pushing it into the wall, and I collapse in the corner, crying quietly but desperately.

'OK, let's go home,' Chelsea Daddy says. 'Little girl just cannot behave herself.'

At the font door, the mistress smiles at me but I cannot smile back.

*

'I'm very proud of you.' In the cab he pulls me towards him, smiling.

'Was I a good girl?'

'Yes, a very good girl.'

I lean my head against his shoulder the whole trip back, utterly exhausted but proud of my performance. When we arrive home, he pays the driver and asks for a receipt. I laugh to myself, wondering how a millionaire could be so cheap; why does he bother claiming it as an expense?

As soon as we enter his bedroom, he takes his penis in his hand and begins masturbating. Kneeling down, I show him my battered and bruised bottom and thighs. He pulls me to his chest and I kiss his face; all the while we're whispering perverted things to each other.

'My worthless little girl, bruised and cut all over her body.'

'Are you satisfied with your little girl's performance?'

'Yes, I'm very satisfied. And I'll rape you soon.'

'I can't wait to be raped by my strict Daddy.'

'I'll finger your smooth shaven pussy, sticking my fingers into your hairless little-girl pussy.'

'And little girl will scream and cry in pain as the blood of the rape will mix with the blood of the caning,' I say, quoting one of his texts.

'How much do you love your Daddy?'

'I love you, Daddy, more than anything. I loved it when you hit me with the thickest cane you could find on the wall at the mistress's. You were cutting my skin so deeply.'

'Did you like it?'

'I did. That was the best part of my Reform School punishment. Can you remember that beautiful, massive thick cane?'

'Was it painful?'

'Did you not hear me whining like a dog?'

'My gorgeous little girl.'

'I'll be your well-cut, well-raped, branded little girl.'

'Ah, ah ...' His heavy sighs mean there is no need to state how much I love the bruises all over my body.

He wipes himself clean, pleased with all the sticky

Torn

stuff that has come out.

Soon after, he is lying on top of me, cuddling me. I can feel his penis near my panties, and then rubbing against my pussy. It's already hard and I'm all wet. How I would love to be free of any underwear as I'm lying under his body right now – my senses are crying out for it so much. But I need to be certain that he has strong feelings for me. I need to save my virginity until I know he loves me.

*

Next morning I make the tea while he is still sleeping. When I return, the TV is on; there is a story on Edinburgh.

'I love that city. It looks so beautiful,' I say, as I place the tray on the bed.

'Ugh, it's terrible! Unfortunately I have to go there every year to make a presentation, but I hate it – so boring. Ugly people, ugly place,' he sneers, sipping his tea.

'What do you mean by ugly people?'

'The people there are just simply ugly. Look at that woman.' He points at the presenter, who is probably in her forties. 'Only young, attractive woman should be allowed to appear on TV. Only pretty ones should appear in the media.'

'But that's discrimination.'

'Everyone really prefers to see stunning, good-looking

people,' he says.

Why is he always judging people on their appearance? I wonder, as I sip my tea.

'How old is your Spanish girlfriend?' I ask curiously, after a long pause.

'Ugh, horrible. Thirty-three. Terribly old.'

'How can you say that?'

'Women are only acceptable under the age of thirty. Over thirty they are degrading, fading away, getting old.'

'So you find her old?'

'And overweight as well.'

'So you find her fat?' I ask, hopeful that I may be able to steal Daddy away from her.

'Not fat, just a bit overweight. I've told her she should go on a diet or do something about it; if she doesn't she will lose me. But she's got a beautiful face – like Penelope Cruz.'

Really? The photo in the living room in which she is cuddling my Daddy on the beach did not remind me of the famous actress. True, she was wearing large sunglasses that hid most of her face, but still ...

'I'll buy her lots of chocolates and sweets to make her happy,' I say sarcastically. He smiles at my suggestion. 'When am I going to see you next?'

'I'm going on holidays for the next few weeks. First with the kids to France, then with the Spaniard to Majorca.'

And what about me? He is taking everyone on holidays: his mother, the kids, even the Spaniard. So what am I? Don't I mean anything to him? Disappointment creeps into my stomach, and I place the teacup back on the tray.

When he pays me my pocket money, I ask him how much he paid for the mistress, and am quite surprised to hear it was four hundred pounds; she hardly did or said anything, and almost all the caning was done by him anyway.

'I think it was a waste of money,' I remark.

'I know. She should have been much stricter,' he says.

'She wasn't even frightening. And to tell you the truth, I preferred it when she was beating me since she didn't cane me brutally like you.'

'She wasn't good enough. I wasn't satisfied with her myself,' he says, seemingly annoyed.

'Don't worry. You more than made up for it. You were very cruel, especially with that thick cane. It was terrible. Like a disaster. I've never had such awful pain.'

'Really? Perhaps I should buy something similar then. Turn around.' He examines the markings on my body but doesn't look entirely pleased. 'That's nothing. Not that bad, but could be much better. You deserve a more severe beating.'

What does he want exactly? Will I ever please him?

On Undefended Flesh

I suffered so much but it's still not enough. He does not even cuddle me; no kisses, no hugs. He says he is in business mode now, getting ready for work, and he applies his eye drops, anti-wrinkle treatment, etc.

'Daddy's driving to work today, so you can come with me for a while. I can take you to Sloane Square.'

When we step out onto the pavement, he has a lot of trouble finding exactly where the car is; it was driven home by his PA, who left a text explaining where she had parked it. Eventually he locates it, and we drive off in silence until we arrive at the station.

'Would you like to say anything to your little girl?' I ask, before getting out. I know it will be a long time till we meet again and I'm expecting him to say something special.

'Be good,' is all he says, and kisses me on the cheek.

*

I recreate the time spent with my Chelsea Daddy while heading home on the bus. It was so marvellous when he was cuddling me in bed last night, but this morning he did not even touch me. I shaved my pussy for him though it did not seem to impress him much. Everyone and everything is more important to him. And now he is going away on holidays again and all he can say is 'be good'. Although I attempt to comfort myself with the notion that I shouldn't get involved with a bastard who considers all women over thirty old, it does not help much – I still love this bastard.

I wait for him to text me during the day, but in the end I have to take the initiative, as usual.

/Where is my Daddy? Why do you ignore your little girl? I'm happy to do any makeover for you, since little girl wants to be exactly what her Daddy wants her to be./

/Just got back from dinner. Can't be around for little girl all the time. But Daddy is pleased his little girl wants to be whatever he chooses. You will be a toilet. Learn to ask to drink Daddy's piss. It's an honour./

Over the next few days I receive no texts or emails – not a thing! I become furious and send him an email with the intention of making him jealous.

Dear Daddy,
Why don't you text your little girl? I did not admit something to you: I went to another master last week and got a pleasant light spanking and discipline. He was very satisfied with me, but was shocked by the sight of the stripes which remained on my thighs after your hard caning and remarked that you abuse me too much.

I am afraid I must look for another master next week as well because my Daddy neglects me. I wanted to be only and exclusively your slave but you do not take my discipline seriously. I do understand that you are busy, but little girl needs regular punishment. You take everyone on holiday – your mum, your kids, your beautiful girlfriend – except your little girl. I just hope that after the holidays you will have more time for my education.

We have not yet explored many things.

You have not seen me in suspenders and whore outfits.

At least text me, please, to keep the humble and obedient slave-fire in me alive. You said I am getting on an upper level in slavery. I do not want to be an average cut girl, I want to be the best one. But to achieve this nice goal I need to have a proper master who treats me as a little piece of shit on a regular basis. So I need your texts, nice bizarre ideas, comments.

Your little girl
Shana@

/**Daddy read your email and is disgusted at the disloyalty. Daddy is SO ANGRY he may have to reject his little girl. He can't even think of any punishment severe enough for such behaviour.**/

This is not the reaction I expected – talking about

rejection. I need to write something more dramatic:

Dear Daddy,

I accept your rejection and regret not being able to try out many more things with you. I do not deserve to be your little girl any more. I have told you several times that you should look for other slave girls because I am not good enough for you. Now I am considering moving back to my country for good.

I really loved our sessions and loved you so much — too much. I was willing to do anything for my Daddy, being under training and doing quite well. I loved you both as a master and as a person. First, I did it only for the money and had many principles that I was not ready to give up; but as time went on I became more and more submissive and accepted your commands in a humble way.

So I wish you a nice holiday with your kids and then with your girlfriend. You were right: I am not fit to be your footstool. Thanks for the sessions, I really enjoyed them. From now on my thighs will be unmarked, and I will throw away the pink ribbon that I bought for next time.

I was your naughty little girl.
Shana@

/Daddy read his little girl's email and will punish her for it. Not only will he feed her

> pee in a baby bottle, but if she will lick up
> Daddy's shit he may reconsider. What does
> little girl say?/

It seems as though the second email has worked better. I do not reply, so he can feel some doubt … so he can taste what I had been feeling.

> /What does my little girl have to say?/
> /Text Daddy, you naughty little girl. You
> haven't replied to me./

But little girl keeps silent for the next few days. He continues to text me, even though by now he is with his kids in France.

> /Because of little girl's naughty email,
> Daddy will give her a nice severe caning on
> the inside of her wet thighs and her smooth
> pussy. He'll then sit his sobbing little girl
> on his lap and read naughty bedtime stories
> while she drinks Daddy's pee from a bottle./

It's getting more and more difficult to not say anything. I try to restrain myself for one more day.

> /Daddy will make his little girl drink his piss
> from a dog's bowl, then he'll take a belt and

whip her breasts. After, she can relax with Daddy and watch DVDs of young girls getting beaten./

/Do you still want your little girl or are you bored with her? You always abandon your little one …/

/Daddy will always want his little girl, but on his terms since he is the boss. You must be patient for your Daddy and respect his strength. Text Daddy with complete devotion and submission./

/I think I should go back to my country, ending my submissive life and turning over a new leaf. Would you like me to go back home?/

/You will not go. You will become my object. I will have a slave contract for you involving cleaning duties in country house and London./

/Do you really need your innocent little girl?/

/Yes, I need my little girl. I can't wait to cane

those innocent little thighs and have her rub my penis with tears in her eyes. Daddy will see his little girl the following Friday for afternoon shopping, makeover and overnight punishment. Also on Saturday for Aston Martin drive to seaside./

/That's great! That goes beyond little girl's wildest dreams. Text me the exact dates, please. Little girl is overjoyed that she can spend a weekend with her Daddy. She can't believe it's true./

/Friday evening 18th till Sun morning 20th. Daddy might even show you country cottage, where you will be suspended for your whippings in the garden. Text me what your little heart desires./

/My little heart wants to be with Daddy. What will we do at the seaside?/

/There will be Aston Martin drive, but after Friday's caning little girl needs to be careful not to get any blood on the seats. Seaside will be lots of treats – smart restaurant, ice creams, cuddles. Then spanking when back in London./

Torn

>/When will you be going on holiday with Spaniard?/

>/Off to Majorca week following our weekend away, Thursday I think. Away for a week, but Daddy will only be thinking of his little girl./

Because my last period was over forty days ago, I begin to get worried. It would be ridiculous – he was rubbing his penis against my pussy, but I was in my panties. There was no blood, so I must still be a virgin.

>/I'm so worried – my period hasn't yet come though it was supposed to arrive a long time ago. You are the only man I've been with. Can you remember when you were on top of me naked? I don't want to be pregnant …/

>/You should buy tester kit from Boots to put your mind at rest. Impossible, there would have been no cum on penis./

He is right, I should make sure. I go to the pharmacy to pick up a kit. Unable to wait, I drink a lot of water in order to pee quickly. Usually it is too easy, but now nothing wants to come. In the end I drink so much that it has no choice. Before checking the result, I close my

On Undefended Flesh

eyes, then open them slowly and sigh with relief: it is negative. So why is my period so late?

A few hours later, however, the familiar pain has arrived, as well as the first drops of blood on my knickers.

By Wednesday night I cannot sleep, just twisting and turning in bed, holding my tummy and pushing the pain with my hands as though trying to push it out. My period feels worse than the cane, which I would prefer to this horrible female disaster. Why couldn't it have come earlier? I'll still be having it when I meet Daddy on Friday. Our first weekend together will be ruined!

*

After finishing work on Friday evening, I catch the bus to Chelsea, feeling incredibly privileged that I get to spend a whole weekend with my Daddy. I bring a couple of bags full of different outfits, ready to impress him. He said we would have a great time together, and I feel this is a brilliant opportunity for us to get closer. I rarely feel as happy as I do now ... Aston Martin drive, seaside, tender moments, not just torture. Nothing can get me down – not even my period.

When I open the door, he's coming down the steps, and I drop my bags and run to him.

'I haven't seen you for such a long time. I was missing

you so much,' I whisper into his ear.

'I won't be away for so long again,' he says with a smile, holding me tight.

'I love you, Daddy. Our first weekend together, I'm so happy that I can be here.'

'My lovely little girl.' He holds my face in his hands and gives me a kiss on my nose. 'First I need to send you for an errand. Go to Partridges and buy a box of cigarettes for your Daddy. Benson and Hedges.' He hands me some cash.

I run to the shop quickly, not only because it has started raining but also as I don't want to miss any precious moments with my Daddy. When I return I sit down on the sofa next to him, smiling at him while stroking his hair, but his face has already turned rigid, emotionless.

'Go to the terrace and stand outside in the pouring rain.' I look at him, surprised, expecting him to express his gratefulness for my errand in an entirely different way, yet do as I am told.

It's raining cats and dogs now. I stand out on the terrace in my jeans and shirt, getting soaked. My eyes are fixed inside the living room but he does not even throw me a glance. He is glued to the screen. He may have even forgotten about his little girl, raindrops rolling down all over her body, making her shiver with cold. Eventually, he looks my way – a face exempt of gesture or emotion – then turns his head back towards the TV after a few seconds.

On Undefended Flesh

Some minutes later he signals with his hand that I can come in.

'Now go upstairs and have a bath before your severe punishment.'

After a hot bath I get dressed into my pink princess dress that I bought during the week. Upon seeing it he appears happy, but his reaction is more muted than when he first saw me in my chequered tunic outfit.

'You're very pretty,' he says. 'Come here.' I get into his lap and he kisses me. I start cuddling passionately, trying to make up for all the cuddles that I've missed while he has been away. Soon though, he reminds me that this weekend won't all be about pleasure.

'Go to the kitchen and bring a wooden spoon from the cupboard next to the fridge. You have to crawl back with the spoon between your teeth.'

A short while later I'm crawling back into the living room. I know that he will want me to remove my panties; taking the spoon out of my mouth, I clear my throat. 'I have to admit something. You'll be very upset – but it's not my fault …' He's looking at me with such intensity, I lose all my strength.

'*What?*'

'I'm having my period.'

He slaps me in the face, hard. I lean down at his feet, begging for his mercy.

'Please! It's not my fault, I cannot control my body. At least I'm not pregnant,' I say, crying at his feet.

'Bend over my knees.' He takes the wooden spoon from my hand and beats me with it on my bottom.

He then devises a new routine for me. First I must crawl around the room with the wooden spoon in my mouth, then he spanks me on his lap and orders me to be his footstool. This keeps repeating until finally he's had enough.

'Go to the bathroom and make a hot bath for Daddy. Make it very deep.'

While the water is running I return quickly to the living room. I want to make sure I get it right.

'Do you want me to put some foam gel into your hot bath?'

'Yes, use the blue bottle.'

When I announce his bath his ready, he walks into the bathroom ... but comes back out, furious. He makes me bend over and beats me hard with the wooden spoon.

'Why?' I cry out, bewildered. 'What's wrong?'

'The bath – not deep enough.' He looks at me angrily, before going back to open the taps.

I watch him as he gets undressed and steps inside the tub. There's so much water in there now that I feel like pushing his big snobby head under and drowning him. He looks so vulnerable, lying there naked without any sparkle in his eyes, absolutely indifferent and numb. I kneel beside him, stroking his naked body gently – his chest, arms, tummy, his legs. Without knowing why, I begin to cry. We are both silent, he stares at me strangely, tears are rolling down my face.

'Are you really a virgin?' he asks.

'Yes. Don't you believe me?'

'Yes, I do.'

My hand is still in the bath, touching him everywhere, everywhere but his penis. He tries to force my hand to touch it, but I pull back.

'You have to learn to touch Daddy's penis.'

He looks at me as my hand slowly reaches for his penis. My eyes remain fixed on his. It's frightening and strange touching my first penis, all the while asking myself why I am doing this? *Another thing he has managed to make me do against my will.*

After he has finished his bath, he tells me to get into position on the bed. He proceeds to cane me, cutting my thighs all over, beating my already bruised bottom to multiply his pleasure and my pain. My screaming and crying do not move him. Eventually, I cannot keep still any longer and move away.

'Accept your punishment properly, otherwise you'll get much more,' he yells.

Resigned to the inevitable, I fix myself in position. He's whipping me not just on my thighs but my soft calves as well. He has become completely senseless – not even granting me a break as the pain becomes unrelenting and never-ending.

Finally, when it's over, he leans down to cuddle me. I run to the window instead, and wrap myself in the curtain as I watch the night lights outside, crying despairingly ...

The pain slowly subsides and I go back to the bed. He puts on a spanking video – a brutal one – of a submissive girl getting beaten by a mistress. I watch the girl with great respect; she does not cry out once, even though her bottom is being beaten more severely than mine. Drops of blood form on the cane but the cruel mistress does not stop. Eventually, the cane is smothered in blood.

My Chelsea Daddy enjoys it very much and starts playing with himself.

'Touch your Daddy's penis.'

Now that I've already touched it, I put my hand on it quickly. I hold it in my hand awkwardly.

'I don't know how to move it.'

'Daddy will show you,' he says, smiling, putting his hand on mine. 'Up and down, up and down,' he keeps repeating.

I do it on my own without his help, whispering '*up and down, up and down ...*' I'm moving his penis gently, trying to obtain a rhythm, waiting impatiently for the sticky stuff to come ... but it does not, making me feel uncomfortable and guilty. *Maybe I'm not doing it right.*

He puts on another video, this time a black and white one: two women again, both are silent and strangely surreal. There are scenes of the sub sucking the dominant woman's heels, hot wax being dropped onto the sub's body, and of course plenty of beatings. At one point the mistress pisses into the sub's mouth, who drinks it, making Daddy very excited.

'This is what really turns me on,' he says while rubbing his penis. He asks for my assistance and I continue with his 'up and down' technique. His orgasm seems to be approaching. He pulls me tight to his chest, whispering his twisted ideas into my head; and I whisper back.

'Little girl will have to drink Daddy's piss. Would you like that?'

'Yes, Daddy's delicious pee will reach my tongue, making me a big girl. Then Daddy will rape me violently.'

'Do you want to be raped violently?'

'Yes. You will be very wild. Forcing your long hard cock inside my hairless, innocent pussy ...'

'Pushing you against the bed, pulling your hair, tying you down to the bed so you can't move. Slapping your face cruelly ...'

'It will be extremely painful for little girl and she'll be crying and screaming, bleeding and suffering for her Daddy all night long.'

'Ah, ah ...'

I turn towards the bedside table to get some tissues.

'Now Daddy's going downstairs to watch TV, have some gin and smoke a bit before coming back to little girl.'

'And what will we do tomorrow?'

'Go to the seaside in Daddy's Aston Martin. I booked a hotel room for tomorrow night.'

'Really!' I become delighted. 'I love you, Daddy.' I cuddle him gently but he does not smile, does not react to my gentle touches at all.

'Come with me to the bathroom.' He takes me by the arm and makes me watch him pee. 'You'll be drinking this from your bottle,' he says.

'Not tonight,' I protest, worried that he really might expect me to.

'No, not tonight ... but very soon. It's an honour to drink Daddy's pee.'

'Yes, it is,' I confirm obediently, feeling disgusted.

He goes downstairs, leaving me alone in his bedroom. Soon I start feeling neglected and abandoned, expecting more from this weekend, especially now that I have touched his penis. I lie on the floor, crying, hungry for love and affection. When finally I hear his footsteps I stand up quickly, waiting for him at the door.

'So now you'll be cuddling and kissing me all night long as you promised me?'

'I'm going to sleep. I'm tired,' he says, disinterested.

'But you promised tender moments. That's unfair,' I say, crying.

'Stop nagging!'

'You lied to me.' I continue to fight for my rights ... for the little portion of love that is due to me.

'You are so irritating right now.' His harsh words

pierce my heart.

'But what shall I do? I touched your penis, received the hard caning. What else can I do to make you happy?'

'Just be nice to me,' he yells, and switches off the lights.

I cannot fall asleep, and so I just lie there quietly, tossing and turning, while he is fast asleep. Questions keep popping up in my head: *What did I do wrong? Why is he acting all weird and cold?*

In the morning I wake at half seven. He's still asleep beside me. I close my eyes, trying to fall back asleep, but cannot. I'm too anxious about our first weekend together.

He wakes at nine. I try to be nice to him – stroking his face, cuddling him, kissing his lips and chest softly – but he does not respond. As he begins watching a cooking programme on the telly, he tells me off.

'I hate it when I'm being stroked. I can't stand it. It's so annoying.'

Then he phones the hotel and cancels the reservation he made for tonight.

'The weather forecast predicts heavy rain later, so there's no point going to the seaside. We may go to Battersea Park instead.'

I feel more and more upset, not being able to understand his behaviour. He is watching TV and reading a glossy magazine, ignoring me completely, as though he was alone in his bed.

'Go and make some tea,' he says eventually.

I go downstairs and prepare his tea. I have trouble concentrating, however, and become nervous that it won't be perfect.

'That's terrible!' he shouts at me, disgusted after taking a sip.

Everything is going wrong. It's already twelve and he's still in bed. I dress into the summer uniform he likes so much, put my hair in bunches and apply some pink lipstick. Looking like a real little girl, I kneel down beside him by the bed.

'Look here,' I say, hoping to get his attention.

He turns his head towards me. 'Pretty,' he says indifferently, before turning back towards the telly.

He's not impressed at all. I try to attract his attention in any way possible. Choosing *Shaven Beauties* and some spanking books from the shelf, I read them next to him, feigning keen interest – but he does not care. I expose my bottom so he can view the bruises and cuts from last night's session – but he does not say a word.

Finally he breaks the silence:

'Why are you here? You are irritating me.'

'But why? What's wrong?'

'You're simply annoying me today. I don't want this, it's better if you go home. Why are you even here at all?'

'It was you who offered this weekend together. Just

you and me. Shopping, seaside, tender moments, kisses, cuddles —'

'Stop it!' he yells. 'I don't want to listen to this crap. I don't feel like being with you today. Go home and leave me alone!'

He goes to the bathroom and I run downstairs, feeling utterly devastated. Hesitating on whether to leave or stay, I decide to hide in the basement. As soon as I enter the slave room, I lie down on the floor, crying desperately but quietly so he will not hear me. Why is this all happening? Why is he acting all strange? The weekend promised so much and started so well — he even promised to never be away from his little girl for so long again — and now ...

As I lie there, I can't help singing along softly to Natalie Imbruglia's song 'Torn'. The lyrics are echoing around in my head and seem to perfectly reflect what I am feeling; little girl's dreams have been *torn* to pieces.

An hour or so later, I approach him and ask if he will let me stay. He is watching *Who Wants to be a Millionaire* and does not bother to look up.

'Go to the kitchen and bring me a bottle of beer.'

I fetch him his drink, and then lie on a couch nearby.

'Why are you so strange today? What's happened?' I ask him.

'I don't want to talk. Shut up!'

After an hour of complete silence, he asks me to go

Torn

on an errand.

'Go to Partridges for a box of cigarettes, same as yesterday, and then to Marks and Spencer to buy some Indian takeaway.'

'And then?'

'Then, you must go home. I know I'm in a strange mood right now, it's weird even for me. But that's the way it is.'

'But why?'

'I don't know. I don't want to talk about it. Go and buy the cigarettes and the food, then go home.'

I get changed into my normal clothes and walk down the street. I feel weak and dizzy; sometimes I bump into people, or they bump into me. It's Saturday afternoon, the sun is out, people are smiling as they shop; and I walk among them, miserable, like a moonwalker, still sorrowful and puzzled by my Chelsea master's behaviour.

When I return I make up a lie, hoping to make him feel guilty.

'I collapsed on the street,' I say, before crying.

'What? Have you eaten anything today?' he shouts at me.

'I haven't had anything for twenty-four hours.'

'Then eat something. Why are you so stupid that you don't even eat, and then you are surprised you pass out on the street,' he continues angrily.

'I don't want to eat. But maybe some milk would be good.'

On Undefended Flesh

'He goes to the fridge to get some milk and offers me some biscuits as well.'

'No, I don't want to eat here. I'll eat at home. Besides, I'm not hungry at all thanks to you.'

'Then go and have some food at home. No wonder you collapse if you haven't had anything.'

He brings me the six hundred pounds.

'I don't need your money!' I cry out hysterically.

He goes to the hall to put it in my bag.

'I'll give it to the first beggar in the street,' I yell.

'You can't do that.'

'I will,' I say, adamant.

He appears very keen to get rid of me. Still sobbing despondently, I ask him to show me his Aston Martin.

'I'll never have another chance to sit in a real one. At least let me have a look.'

He leads me to the garage and we both sit inside the stunning green vehicle. It's such an amazing machine, but I cannot even concentrate on it: all I can do is imagine how incredible it would have been to drive to the seaside with my Daddy.

'Stop crying, please,' he says.

'Haven't you realised yet, it's all because of you! Why is it so surprising that I'm crying after this terrible day?' I ask him, furious, struggling through my tears.

He takes me to the front door. 'Text me when you get home and have had something to eat,' he says.

'Why do you pretend to care for me when you don't?

Thanks for this *lovely* weekend. I enjoyed every moment of it. *You are a fantastic Daddy!*'

He does not say a word, just closes the door behind me.

10

Little Girl's Broken Heart

I walk along the streets, heartbroken. After making my slow way home, I send a text to assure him I have eaten – though I have not, having no appetite at all.

> **/Good. Yes, still want to be your Daddy. Daddy will feel better soon./**

The next day I write him an email.

> *Dear Daddy,*
> *Your worthless adopted daughter doesn't understand what's going on. She made your tea, stood outside in the rain, and offered her pure bottom for a brutal*

Little Girl's Broken Heart

caning.

For some reason you just changed your mind about our weekend together. You told me off for being annoying, but I was just upset because you didn't keep your promise and I didn't know what I did wrong. And I still don't know.

I just feel that you are bored with me. If it's true you should let me know, so I can serve other masters. I do take my discipline and punishment seriously. I want to be dedicated to only one master. And I also need a Daddy. Even if you don't need me any more I would like to be your friend and keep in touch, though I would rather be your slave or little girl because I feel more comfortable in these roles.

I was crying on Saturday because I felt ashamed. You were not impressed by my school uniform, my bunches, my lipstick. I just don't know why you have changed so much. I am still the former little girl with her genuinely submissive, obedient and humble nature who wants to be Daddy's worthless little adopted daughter. Nothing more, nothing less. But something has happened to Daddy ...

I want to get back the old Daddy. Your little girl wants to see you again. She cannot get you out of her head.

I don't want to lose you.
I don't want you to refuse me.
I don't ask for much.

Just a little piece of you, that is all I need.
Just please don't ignore me.
I cannot give up being your little girl. This notion has been planted deep inside my mind and my soul by you, Daddy.
Your naughty little girl
Shana@

A few days go by and I still haven't heard from him. I decide to post a new ad on www._____

GOOD GIRL LOVES BEING USED AND ABUSED AND EXPLOITED

Nice young innocent girl with a variety of school uniforms offers her pure white thighs and bottom for spanking, brutal caning, whipping, beating or whatever. No sexual favours offered, anything else considered.

She especially loves verbal humiliation and she will make all your aspects of fantasy (even perverted ones — she is quite used to them) come true. Please note, she cannot accommodate so you must provide the venue where the exclusive session will take place.

She is a professional and intelligent spankee looking for similar types of masters. She is humble and obedient by nature so you will not be disappointed by her. No time wasters, please. Only mature, expert men who know exactly what they want should apply.

Little Girl's Broken Heart

*

/Hi. I am from Kenton, North London, and would like to give you a spanking over my knee by hand and ruler. Also would like to cane you. I am experienced and a good strict spanker./

The ruler makes me smile, but I delete the message, just like all the others coming in, realising no one is going to impress me as much as my Chelsea master.

/Hi. I am in East Grinstead. We can do any scenario – prisoner, schoolgirl, maid, etc. I am experienced. Would pay £200 an hour or more if punishment was hard (but no blood)./

/Can we meet this weekend, Saturday or Sunday, so that I can beat, whip and brutally cane your white thighs and bottom? I want to prove that I'm not a time waster./

/Hello. John here. 54-year-old man, very experienced in discipline, spanking, caning, toilet training, humiliation. Would love to meet you. Interested?/

(Not really …)

On Undefended Flesh

> /I arrange CP parties, where 3 or 4 girls who enjoy CP are made to confess their sins, and up to 6 guys spank, strap, flog and cane them in front of the group./

I am a private spankee – not a party animal. And anyway, I do it for money, not for fun.

One man becomes angry when I do not reply to his text:

> /If you keep me waiting too long, I will beat you with one of the whips I use to correct my horse when it misbehaves. There are several kinds of horse whips I can use on you. Contact me any time during the day or night to show me that you want to be a good girl./

I doubt if I will. But he carries on.

> /Be a good girl and I will give a present to spend on yourself. Get in touch with me before I change my mind./

(You can change your mind, I will not be upset.)

> /I'm 27. Hammersmith. Clean. Require school dress or French maid outfit. Will pay your rate. Bring a whip. Up for it?/

He does not text back after I inform him my going rate. Not that I mind; he sounds like an inexperienced butt-head, asking me to bring a whip when it is the master's duty to provide the implements. Besides, he is far too young – twenty-seven! – he could not be my Daddy.

> /I will take you to the dungeon for 2 hours. You will be stripped and put over my knee to receive a hard spanking to your thighs and bottom. You will then be tied to a St Andrew's cross and I will use 2 different floggers on your breasts. To finish, I will attach nipple clamps and secure you to a whipping bench, where I will use my dragon bamboo cane on your bottom. Tell me what would be your fee?/

It sounds frightening (and exciting) … but nipple torture?

> /My Chelsea master pays me £600 per session without nipple torture./

> /I would pay £600 but it would have to include nipple torture. So get in touch if you ever change your mind. The money is waiting in my pocket./

On Undefended Flesh

I forward the previous text to my Chelsea Daddy, hoping that he might become a little jealous. He does not reply. So I send another text with the sweet little lie that I have ordered the spanking DVDs for him. This trick seems to work, as he responds immediately.

> **/Good girl for ordering DVDs. Go to www⎯⎯⎯ and choose two more, not Neighbour, Stalin, Warlock's Revenge, Reform School 2 or 8th Commandments. Text me with what children's accessories you suggest and would like./**

*

It's Thursday. I'm lying in bed watching the planes in the sky, thinking of my Chelsea Daddy who is flying to Majorca today with his girlfriend. Whenever a plane appears I think it might be the one, and my heart breaks into little pieces as I imagine them together. I'm crying, feeling extremely jealous and lonely.

*

Hi Shana,
It's Pete. I thought you might like an email since I can put down a lot more detail than I ever could in a text. This also gives you my private email address so you can reply or contact me anytime. You might like to print some of the details as a guide for our session next Wednesday 30th Aug.

Little Girl's Broken Heart

A bit about me first. I'm a genuine business executive, 51, quite well off, and educated in 3 universities. I travel around a lot, both in the UK and abroad, and have been in the spanking scene for about 14 years. In all that time I've met some great female spankees, and never had any complaints over any session I've been involved in.

I'm very experienced in the discipline scene and would normally play out scenarios. In your particular case, this will be student/tutor; however, I will also discipline you exactly as the person you are — 24-year-old Shana — whenever it is necessary. I take firm control of every session, but you can trust me to always stay within our agreed terms.

In order that you get an idea of my approach to discipline, listed below are 10 general guidelines on how I think and operate. It saves you guessing, but you don't have to remember them all at once. I will help you do them in our first sessions, and then over time they will become second nature:

1) Accepting Real Discipline.
As stated above, part of any session may involve my punishing you just as you are — Shana, age 24. This happens if there is a real reason. For example: my previous text offered you well-intentioned advice to be careful when sharing your work details. This was based on my experience — but not really treated seriously

enough by you. Shana *was perhaps just a little too stubborn? If I, as a tutor, give advice, I expect you, as student, to respectfully consider it. Therefore, part of next Wednesday may be spent punishing you as a reminder of this.*

Other possible reasons you might get disciplined as Shana *are, for example, if my texts don't ever get an answer or get impolite answers, or you are late turning up to one of our sessions. You get the idea.*

When you are disciplined as yourself no dressing up is needed and it is usually just a brief introduction to the full session. The punishment is given while you are wearing jeans, skirt or punishment skirt (see item 10 below).

2) Being Ready for the Scenario
Apart from any discipline you earn for yourself under item 1, most of the session will be an imagined scenario. I want you to continue the student theme and take the role of a school/college student in mid to late teens (age 16/17). This may involve some immature behaviour, but not as far as that of a very young girl. I identify most closely with the need for naughty teenagers and young adults to be disciplined, as it is more shameful for them. Your school uniforms can be used in this scenario, but, for me, you should not dress to appear too young.

Little Girl's Broken Heart

3) Dressing Modestly
Apart from your uniform, I am particular about some other aspects of a spankee's clothing, especially underwear. You should, for example, always wear plain panties which fully cover your bottom. I will take a poor view if you are wearing anything too glamorous — like a thong — because you need to show your basic modesty and shyness.

I also would like you to wear jeans or a tight fitting skirt when you are not dressed for a scenario. Ideally, you will wear jeans and bring the skirt with you as a possible punishment skirt, along with your uniform. Later I may get you a proper punishment skirt (see item 10 below).

4) Offering Your Bottom Submissively
It is very important that you offer your bottom properly for discipline. I will help you with this, but basically in any bent over position you must slightly arch your lower back and shoulders so that your back forms a gentle U-shape from bottom to shoulders. This body posture gives good submissive signals from you to me, and has the desired effect of pushing your bottom outwards for my attention.

5) Other Body Postures
Your body language needs to show humility and sorrow as you are being disciplined. When you are standing

On Undefended Flesh

upright, a simple rule to follow is to keep your bottom as outwards as possible and your head tilted downwards in shame. This can be practiced in front of a mirror. Also, it is a good idea to try and have your eyes avoid mine, particularly when being lectured.

6) Psychology and Mind
Discipline sessions are always partly experienced in the head. Therefore, my sessions allow for lots of corner time, as well as being lectured, shamed or humiliated by verbal comment. You need to feel and show me how ashamed you are with being punished at your sensitive age by a man. To have your pants taken down IS humiliating, and you can plead with me to be spared this indignity, or you can express your shame by, for example, groaning, crying, covering your face with your hands, etc.

7) Accepting the Punishment
Normally the sessions will start and finish over my knee, as this is the most reassuring punishment for a girl and a good way for her to show she wants to make amends. In between, there will be a succession of more formal beatings with different positions and implements (including cane, American paddle, tawse/strap, slipper, hairbrush).

Although you should feel free to cry and show me you are sorry, it is important that you feel you deserve the punishment and push your bottom up in cooperation.

8) Showing Your Genuine Reactions
I expect you to show your shame or pain by body language, words, cries, tears, etc. These reactions must always be genuine, never false or over-dramatised. I am not interested in 'pretend' reactions at all and punish girls severely who do this.

As a safety measure, I offer all spankees a safe word to use if they are close to reaching the end of their limits (though as I can read their reactions well, few have ever had to use it). If ever I hear you say the word 'Budapest', the session will stop immediately. The safe word is deliberately chosen as something which would rarely be said in ordinary speech, and Hungary's capital city is an obvious one for you. If you don't want to have a safe word, that's ok too, but this is one of the few choices I will give you in a session.

9) Wanting to Please
I like spankees who are keen to please and, just as important, find ways to show this. So although she may appear nervous when told her punishment, the spankee might nevertheless say she deserves it and wants to accept all the strokes as best she can. A nice touch (to be used sometimes, not every time) is to ask for extra strokes to remove your guilt, or to tell the master you have let him down and ask to be punished to wipe the slate clean.

10) Understanding Her Buttocks Must Always Be Available
For good, solid master/spankee relations, the spankee must understand and demonstrate that during any session her buttocks are entirely at her master's call.

When I am punishing you as Shana, I might like to pay for you to have a special punishment skirt for this purpose. The item is best in tasteful leather (cheap versions in PVC are not suitable for a good girl like you). The front is suitably modest and conceals the spankee's privates, but the back holds her bared buttocks on display, making it available for her master at his choosing. Therefore, the skirt emphasises a girl's submissiveness whenever it is worn and puts all the focus on her bottom, which is exactly where it should be.

So that tells you about our sessions and how they are likely to go. Once they are over I may decide to attend to your bottom, possibly with cream, so that you are not unnecessarily bruised the next day. This is up to me to decide, depending on my judgement of how your bottom has taken the punishment.

Then, with the punishment over, I like to revert to just being Pete and Shana, finishing the time with a drink, nice conversation, and a bite to eat in a local restaurant. This is optional but always offered, and it pleases me if you are able to accept. It shows there are

Little Girl's Broken Heart

good feelings between us after the session and that we stay friends. We also arrange the next meeting before we leave the restaurant.

And remember: I am never brutal, always firm, always approachable, so we can discuss things between us. Above all, this is a long email for the good reason that I want you to know how I will punish you. Please send a brief email back letting me know any thoughts.

Best wishes and looking forward very much to meeting you next week.

Pete@

And the following day:

Hi Shana,
I'd also like to briefly outline the student/tutor scenario for our upcoming session. You should find it interesting, tense, and very suitable for your uniforms. You will be a young Hungarian student attending a very strict English boarding school for girls at a time many years ago. I will be the Headmaster. The scenario will involve your first ever strict punishment as a student in this strange country of England with its (for you) unfamiliar approach to the corporal punishment of young girls.

By the way, have you had any personal knowledge of corporal punishment as it operated in Hungary? Did you ever experience it there? Know anybody who did?

> *Was it much used in schools or homes or disciplinary establishments during your childhood? I can build anything you have knowledge of (or even just an inkling about) into the scenario, and it can make it seem more realistic for you. So let me know.*
> *Pete@*

(Umm ... not too sure if I'd like to make it more realistic.)

I text him back my lack of knowledge; though, not wanting to discourage him, I thank him for his emails.

> **/Glad you like emails. Not only will they serve as a guide, but will remind you I am noting any naughtiness and thinking of how Shana's bottom will make amends. I am medium height, quite powerfully built, ex-sports player, strong arms and chest, fair hair, shaved, glasses. Smart. Pete./**

*

Oh, very smart! I remark to myself when I see him approaching: a short, overweight, balding, unattractive man with a great big smile. But that's okay; he may not be as charming as my Chelsea master, but at least I'm not going to fall in love with him and burn my heart like I did with my Daddy.

He requires a relaxed chat before the session, so we

go to the bar of the hotel for a drink. We sit on a sofa; he drinks his wine, I sip on water.

'I've tried one hundred and thirty-five spankees so far from all around the world – mainly Australian, American and English girls,' he says.

'How do you know the exact number?'

'Look. I keep a diary of them.' He shows me a notebook with a long list of names and contact numbers.

'That's incredible,' I say, astonished. 'I assume I will be the first Hungarian in your collection.'

'You will be,' he says, with a smile.

He continues on, talking about how he's divorced with three grown-up kids, but now has a new partner who satisfies him sexually and knows all about his spanking visits.

We make our way upstairs.

'You know that the safe word is "Budapest". So whenever you think it is above your limits just let me know by saying the safe word and I will stop. All right?'

He looks very pleased when I come out of the bathroom in my uniform, but he sends me back to knock on the door from the inside since we are now officially in the headmaster's office.

I knock on the door, waiting for his answer.

'Who's that?' he asks, in a posh, formal manner.

'It's Shana. I was asked to report to you.'

'Come in.'

On Undefended Flesh

I come out of the bathroom.

'So you're Shana, our new student.'

'Yes, Sir.' I turn my head down, avoiding his eyes.

'Stand in front of me,' he says, from his position on the sofa. 'So why do you have to report to me today, Shana? Are you perhaps finding it difficult to settle into our school?' he says theatrically, wanting to prompt me.

Obviously he is fond of role playing, building up the scene so as to create a certain atmosphere. I'm not so keen but force myself to act. It would be much easier if we could just move on, and Shana can take her beating without having to act as though she were on stage.

'There are certain problems with my behaviour. I've done some mischievous things.'

'What have you done exactly?' He looks at me with an exceptionally strict face.

'During lunch I was smoking outside the school with some other girls. I was caught reading a magazine in geography, was late for PE lessons, and I constantly forget about my maths homework.'

'Well, lots of sins to confess. And we can't forget that you've come all the way from Hungary to learn and develop yourself in our superior college. I don't think your parents will be too pleased to discover their little girl has been wasting away her education. Do you?'

'No, Sir,' I say, nodding my head.

'You should be making better use of your time spent

here, instead of misbehaving. Shouldn't you?'

'Yes, Sir.'

'Now, I need to decide on which disciplinary action to choose as a punishment – either to expel you from the boarding school or impose a severe physical punishment. Which option would you prefer?'

'I'm ready to take any punishment, but don't ban me from the school, please,' I tell him, getting down on my knees, begging to be allowed to stay in that imaginary school of his.

'I might be generous and give you one last chance to stay. But then, you have to be severely punished. *Do you understand?*'

'Yes, I do.'

'You forgot something.'

'Yes, I do, *Sir*.'

'That's better. Now take off your panties and bend over my knees.' I lie across his legs and he begins spanking my bottom. 'Naughty girl, insolent troublemaker. You have to learn how to behave. This boarding school has no place for this type of behaviour. Do you understand?'

'Yes, I do, Sir,' I reply obediently, as he hits me with his strong hands.

'Now I'll show you the implements that I'm going to use on you to make you a good girl.' He stands up and points to the table. 'An American strap, a slipper, a belt and a cane.'

I look at them without surprise, familiar with all of them.

'You can choose one for your first punishment.'

I pick the strap. (It seems the least objectionable.)

'Bend over the back of the sofa,' he says, and proceeds to hit me with the strap. 'This is for smoking outside the school. You have to learn that you are not allowed to smoke.'

When the strapping is over, he gently strokes my bottom, which really irritates me — the punishment being far preferable to those soft touches.

For the next stage of the beating I choose the belt, which will be my punishment for reading magazines during geography. He makes me stand by the wall with my arms lifted. He beats me hard but not enough to trigger my tears. Again it is followed by that irritating massage.

Soon it's the slipper's turn. I have to get in a new position on the bed, exposing my bottom high.

'Well, Shana. Will you ever be late again for PE lessons?' He's always talking, always making me affirm his statements, which is getting rather tedious.

'No, Sir, I won't. I'll always arrive on time, Sir.'

'Good girl.'

He carries on hitting me with the slipper, causing me to moan and make some noise since it is getting quite painful. I'm hoping that he may have forgotten about my last sin ... but his memory works just fine.

'Now choose the last implement that I must use on you for forgetting your maths homework.'

There is nothing left on the table to choose – only the cane. He has me bend over the table and starts caning me hard. I look behind to see his face growing with excitement as each successive blow is harder than the last. Turning the other way, I'm instead confronted by my image reflected in the mirror ... and him again, whipping me with enthusiasm, sighing with joy and relief. He's almost running out of breath as he uses all his strength.

The pain increases and I cry out, thinking how unlucky I am that I should be here. I should have been with my Daddy, discovering Majorca hand in hand, making passionate love with him every night. *Why couldn't it have been me?* I look back. He's trying to beat me even harder, as though he wants me to use the so-called safe word – but I stay strong. Only when he sees the tears rolling down my face does he let up.

'All right, Shana? I think you've learned your lesson today. I hope you will become a good girl after this severe punishment.'

'Yes, Sir. Thank you for punishing me in order to improve my personality and make me a good girl. I promise from now on I'll be a spotless example to my other classmates,' I say, through tears.

After I have changed out of my uniform, he praises my

performance.

'You took your punishment perfectly, cried out, acted the scenario in a brilliant way. You were excellent – in my top three spankees ever.'

'Really ... What were your other spankees like?'

'Well, unfortunately most of them are bored during the session: just come in, take the beating, don't even cry, or, what's worse, pretend to cry. They don't show any interest or emotion. It's obvious they do it only for the money. But you're one hundred percent genuine.'

He wants to take me out for dinner to a classy restaurant. But I refuse his offer politely, pretending to have an early shift at work the next day.

'Before I give you the fee, I'd like to spank you in your jeans as Shana, the person – not the schoolgirl in uniform for the sake of a role play, but you, as you are. All right?'

He's the first client to come up with this idea and I don't like it; it's as if he wants the punishment to reach deeper. There is a kind of metamorphosis that takes place when I get dressed: the obedient girl in the uniform is not exactly the same as the girl who finally gets away with the cash. But now he wants to beat the *real* me, not just the commercial submissive.

Just wanting to get it over with, since the session has already passed two hours, I reluctantly bend over his knees, letting him spank me over my jeans. I close my eyes to hide the disgust clearly evident on my face, and when I open them again it is all over and I receive my payment.

'I'll give you two hundred pounds because you really deserve it. You did work for that amount, Shana, and I'm happy to pay you extra.'

'Thank you.' I drop a weak smile, looking at the money which is fifty pounds more than what we agreed.

'I hope we can meet again soon, as I want you to be my regular spankee. All right?'

He insists on accompanying me to the bus stop. Fortunately a bus soon arrives, and I quickly hop on, waving goodbye to my enthusiastic, but rather annoying, companion.

*

/Daddy wants his little girl to come over this Friday 7.30. Text back./

/Do you want me to stay overnight?/

/Little girl will stay overnight. Daddy wants answer on DVD choice. We could have a cinema evening./

/Little girl has to admit she hasn't yet ordered DVDs. She will do so soon./

/Doesn't sound very respectful to your

On Undefended Flesh

Daddy. You will be put in your place Friday. You won't be able to sit down for a week./

On Friday, I work in the store between seven and five, and then hurry home to shower and get myself fresh for Daddy. My bottom is still bruised somewhat, though I have little time to worry about it since I'm running late. By the time I turn into his street it's already half hour past the appointed time. I receive his text on the doorstep.

/I assume you are not coming so I'm going to make other plans./

That's unfair! I push down on his doorbell frantically. The door clicks open. He's coming down the staircase, looking elegant and charming in a suit and tie, even though he has a strict look on his face.

'You're late,' he says angrily.

'I do apologise.' I look at him with desperate eyes. He does not hug me. It's all different now; no more greetings of gentle cuddles, soft kisses on my cheeks and tender smiles. All I get is that rigid look.

We go to the living room.

'Get on the floor,' he commands, before I can even get changed. I kneel down in my jeans, moving under his legs to become his footstool.

'Lick my shoes.' I lick his shoes diligently while he

Little Girl's Broken Heart

watches TV, even licking the soles to show him my complete obedience. Yet he still looks cold and indifferent, not saying anything. The silence is embarrassing.

'Take off your jeans,' he says finally.

'Could you not beat me today? Please, Daddy! Let's watch spanking movies instead.' I implore him on my knees, but he becomes suspicious.

'Take off your jeans and show me your bottom,' he says firmly.

I give up on begging any further and slowly pull down my jeans. He pulls down my knickers, revealing my bruised bottom. I turn back, looking at him, ashamed.

'What's this?' he asks furiously.

'I hit myself when I bumped into a cage at work. I was unloading the morning delivery –'

'That's ridiculous. It's obvious you were spanked.'

'No, believe me, Daddy.'

'Shut up!' he screams.

To my immense relief and surprise, however, his fury soon dies down.

'Let's go upstairs. I'll show you the video I made with the American girl.'

The film was made in the same bedroom, on the same bed. I cannot see her face since she is in the beating position I am usually in. She exposes her bottom and Daddy beats her with a cane. She is screaming and crying. He goes to cuddle her and encourage her gently: 'Let Daddy

On Undefended Flesh

beat you some more. Be a good girl, Daddy's little girl.'

He continues whipping her ... but the session seems milder than those he does with me, and he appears to be nicer, constantly motivating her with tender hugs. She is going mad, hiding her head under the pillows. Daddy now stops beating her and starts caressing her body gently.

He stops the tape.

'Why did you stop it?'

'We'll watch something else instead,' he says.

'Did you have sex with her after the beating?'

'Yes, we did.'

'Did you record it with the camera?'

'Yes, it was also filmed.'

'And you don't want me to see it.'

He smiles and puts on another video. A girl dressed in school uniform is being caned hard by a mistress. The beating continues long after the cane has been stained with blood and her bottom and thighs have turned shockingly red. Daddy gets aroused and lies back on the bed rubbing his penis, taking my hand to it. I move his penis up and down like he showed me. Soon he ejaculates his sticky stuff, and wipes it off with the tissues I fetch him.

He's lying on the bed, eyes closed. I watch him for a while.

'What happened that weekend when you sent me

home?'

'I know, I was very funny.'

'Not only funny – but strange and frightening as well.'

'I was just depressed.'

'But I don't understand. On Friday night everything went well. Then you woke up on Saturday morning ...'

'I woke up on Saturday and suddenly I started to feel guilty ... because of the Spaniard. The following week we were to go on holiday, and I planned the weekend with you. I just felt guilty.'

'But you always have girlfriends at the same time.'

'Yes – I've got a complicated life.'

'And what about me?'

'You were a maybe relationship – but you go bonkers all the time with your mood swings and get too emotional. Actually, all women go bonkers, I don't understand how you females can stand each other at all ... Let me show you something.'

He goes upstairs, returning shortly with a small yellow book in his hand and a big grin on his face. He hands it to me.

'I got this book from a friend of mine. Designed for men like me who don't understand women.'

I glance at the title: *All You Know about Women*. Opening it, I discover there are only empty pages. I smile and hand it back to him ... though the smile quickly disappears off my face:

'I think it's better if you go home now. Perhaps we can meet when I get back from the US.'

'When?'

'I don't know, I'll text you. Maybe the week after next.'

I give him a hug and leave, feeling sad and disappointed, knowing I've lost the game to the Spaniard. If only I didn't love him so much ...

*

But my crazy flame only grows stronger. That night before going to bed, I text him.

> /Little girl loves her Daddy. You are a great man./

> /You are great too. Good night for now./

Throughout the weekend I continue to send him texts. But he does not respond, making me nervous as well as angry.

> /Little girl is missing her Daddy. She is longing for Daddy's severe punishments. I am begging for a brutal beating./
> /Your pee will be my morning tea, your shit is my lunch, your sticky stuff my shower gel during the evening bath./

/Do you still want your little girl? I may move back to my country for good. Would you like that?/

/I don't know. We'll talk when we meet. You're getting too intrusive right now./

Why did I believe in him so much? He always warned me not to become emotional, but I can't control my feelings – can't help falling in love with him.

My sorrow increases further the next day.

/So when would you like to discipline your little girl again?/

/Difficult to say. Have increased obligations with girlfriend./

It strikes me through the heart. What does he mean by 'increased obligations'? I feel terrified, shocked and lost. What's happened? Is she pregnant? I soon get my answer:

/She's moving in./

'*She's moving in*'! Two weeks ago he was cuddling *me*, calling *me* his little girl; and now he is moving in with someone he hardly mentions, and, if he does, simply refers to as 'the Spaniard'.

I phone him.

'What's going on? How come you've decided this all of a sudden?'

'It's been in the air for a while now. I just want to give it a chance and see how it goes.'

'She probably wants marriage and kids and –'

'No, she doesn't want to marry, and doesn't want children.'

'But you want to marry her and become a committed man? – Is she good in bed?'

'Well, quite good.'

'But she doesn't let you cane her?'

'No.'

'And how will you be able to live without caning, humiliation and all those nasty things you do to me?'

'We can still meet, but it may be a bit more complicated. I just need a break for now.'

'What about me? What do you think of me?'

'I don't know. I find you sexy and intriguing, but you're also emotionally unstable.'

'Does she love you?'

'Yes, she does.'

'Do you love her?'

'I'm not sure. She's a nice girl and we'll see how it goes.'

'I'm so upset now. I'm losing my Daddy and I can't do anything.'

'I'll contact you later ... bye.'

He hangs up and I burst out crying.

The next few days I can barely eat, having no appetite at all, not even for sweets or chocolate. When I try and force some food down, my digestive system remains absolutely resistant, making most of it end up in the sink. The worst part is, I have no one with whom I can share my grief. What would be the point anyway? What could I possibly say: *'I've lost my Daddy'? 'My Chelsea master does not want to cane me anymore'?*

Perhaps if it had been the other way round, if I had ditched him, it would not feel so painful. But now it feels humiliating. Even though he thinks she's overweight and too old, he prefers her to me. What does she know that I don't? *Why am I always rejected by men?* ... My world has collapsed completely and I cannot see the light at the end of the tunnel.

*

It's a Wednesday. I have the day off work and have made an appointment to see Pete. (It has to be better than crying all day in bed.)

We meet at Bayswater tube station again. He looks excited when he recognises me but all I can manage is a faint, drawn smile. When we get to the hotel I cannot hold back my tears, pouring out every detail of my great disappointment to him. He seems compassionate, even

On Undefended Flesh

asking if I would like to cancel the session. Eventually, however, I manage to hold back my tears and compose myself long enough to go ahead with the role play.

In today's scenario I am a prisoner and he is the judge. I've been sentenced to jail for bringing drugs into the UK from abroad. He punishes me in various ways – the strap, slipper, cane and his firm hands – but though I'm trying hard to participate, I am almost zombie-like in my performance.

He sends me to the window and makes me stand there with my hands above my head. The curtains are not fully drawn, so I gaze outside at the mass of people passing by ...

If only I could have a normal life like them, just walking in the streets, shopping, socialising, making friendships, maybe studying something so I can broaden my mind. Why instead do I visit strange men who pay money to beat and humiliate me? What is the point in this? Here I am in this ridiculous drama school session with a man who grates on my nerves, who wants me to affirm his constant questions – 'all right?', 'do you understand?' –

'Take off your panties.'

I throw them on the carpet. He walks over and stomps on them with his shoes. Immediately I become furious and lose my submissive mind.

'Don't stand on my panties! It's unhygienic!' I yell.

But he does not move; he's trying to squash them

deeper into the carpet.

'Why am I not allowed to stand on your knickers? What's going to happen?'

'I just don't like it. I don't want to catch some *disease*.'

He slaps me on the face. Now he too is furious.

'Get dressed and go away. I don't need you if you can't even tolerate my standing on your knickers.'

I lean down to pick up my clothes, but he suddenly has a change of heart, asking me to stay.

'Go on the bed and bend over the pillow. You need to be caned for your insolence.'

Obediently I bend over. He begins beating me very hard. I look back to see his face fuelled with anger, the caning now a revenge for my outburst. His eyes are becoming bigger — I can even see his teeth as he beats me, grinning all the while. He is losing all self-control, the strokes getting harder and harder. When it has reached the levels of my Chelsea sessions, I cry out:

'You are beating me too brutally. You can't do it. Only my Chelsea master can beat me so hard.'

'Ah, but *he's* exceptional.'

'He's unique! No one can go near him!' I say, crying despairingly.

'But *he* rejected you. *He* doesn't want you any more.'

Maybe I could put up with the physical pain, but I cannot bear these cruel words which batter my already broken heart, causing me to scream and cry hysterically.

I get up from the bed.

'YOU ARE ONLY A FAR CRY FROM MY CHELSEA DADDY!' I scream into his face.

He begins roaring wildly.

'That's ENOUGH! Go home and I never want to see you again. *Stupid Hungarian bitch!'*

'I'm going home. I've had enough of these stupid sessions. Give me the money and I'll get out of this place,' I say, dressing into my jeans.

'I'm not going to pay you, as you haven't done your job.'

'You can't do that!'

'Yes I can.' He's looking at me with a cold, ironic grin.

'Then I'll go downstairs and talk to the receptionist. I'll show him my bottom. Maybe he can call the police to sort it out.' I threaten him with my only weapon.

His anger seems to quickly abate.

'Shana, stop it. Yes, of course I'll pay you. I just got angry, but we can't finish the session like this. I have to spank you over your jeans as Shana, the twenty-four-year-old girl who works in a store. All right?'

'No, I don't want it! Give me the money and I'm going home now.'

'Shana, you're a very good spankee. Why do you have to spoil it all? Come on, let's finish it properly. *All right?'* he says, his irritating expression ringing in my ears.

Wanting the ordeal to be over, I finally relent. He

spanks me a few times over my jeans, then pays me the money.

He wants me to stay for a chat, but I want to escape immediately.

'Shana, please don't run away. I still want to be your friend and your client. Is that all right?'

'Please stop, *all right?* I've got to go now.'

'Shana, wait!'

Ignoring him, I run outside into the corridor and head for the nearest lift. But he won't give in.

'Shana, can I come with you to the bus stop?' he asks, following me.

'No, thank you. I'll find my own way.'

'I didn't want to hurt you. I'm sorry if I was too harsh. Let's stay friends. All right?'

My nerves are going to pieces. *If I hear that expression one more time ...*

'Let me breathe, please. ALL RIGHT!'

A sad, hurt expression forms on his face. He turns back without saying another word.

I get into the lift. 'Let's go home,' I tell myself, *'all right?'*

11

Mick's Bitch

The next few days go by slowly and desperately. Somehow I manage to hold it together at work despite always fighting back tears and feeling weak from being unable to eat. I receive plenty of text messages but they do not cheer me up since they are not from my Daddy.

> /Hi Shana. Can you get back to me on visiting you? I don't want to lose touch with an excellent spankee like you. Pete./
> /Will you offer me your bottom after two weeks? I think it will be time you went over my knee again. And I'll be fair this time./
> /Shana, am I still a master you would like

to see again? I need more access to your Hungarian bottom. Will pay well. I have a good sense of humour and am smiling over this./

I do not respond to his texts, which increasingly irritate me as I wait for a sign from my Daddy. But Daddy remains silent. He's a committed man now, living with his girlfriend – he does not need his little girl any more. Two whole weeks have passed since I saw him last, and I cannot restrain myself any longer.

/Little girl is missing her Daddy. Her bottom and thighs are so pure and unmarked. Her body is a sculpture which needs further carving by Daddy./

/If Daddy invites his little girl over soon, what state will her bottom and thighs be in afterwards?/

/Little girl will be beaten black and blue. When would you like to punish your naughty little girl next?/

/Monday evening 7-10pm. You are clearly overdue a severe whipping. Will little girl look forward to her beating?/

On Undefended Flesh

/Little girl is very excited about her next punishment. What scenario would you prefer?/

/Daddy's going to beat little girl with a wooden spoon until her skin breaks, and then cut her thighs with a cane. Will repeat three times during the evening. You will take months to recover./

/It sounds frightening./

/You will thank Daddy from the tears of your torture. All little girls should feel the cut of the cane. Now Daddy's going to sleep./

The whole weekend I feel delighted. No more vomiting food into the sink, crying at night; I can sleep, smile again. Even if the session is only commercial, I will at least be with him.

/Daddy wants you to buy grey tunic-style dress and proper white school panties for your punishment. You can get both from Peter Jones. Have hair in bunches./

*

Before my Monday session begins, I pop into the huge

department store to buy the uniform he requested. The appointment is at seven, but by six I'm already ringing his bell, hoping that my early arrival will mean more time with Daddy. There's no answer, however. He's probably at work or on the way home. I don't want to disturb him with a text, so I sit on the front steps waiting for him patiently. The street of magnificent snow-white buildings is peaceful and marvellous, like usual. I watch as the wind sweeps the fallen autumn leaves between the elegant sports cars parked on the side of the road, daydreaming about how great it would be to live here with my Daddy. But I become upset when I realise that it is the Spaniard who can call this wonderful place her home.

I've been sitting there for thirty minutes when my phone beeps.

/Come in./

That brief text shocks and disappoints me. So all along he's been inside, probably watching from the window, but preferred to leave his little girl out in the cold.

He lets me in and comes downstairs, looking at me angrily. I'm angry too:

'I can't believe it. You're home and you didn't let me in.'

'I said seven. You didn't arrive on time. If I say seven, come at seven, not any earlier, not later. I'll punish you for not being punctual.'

On Undefended Flesh

'I do apologise, but I went to Peter Jones and finished shopping earlier than I thought. That's why I got here so early. I'm sorry for it.'

'Get changed, put on the new uniform and come to the living room.'

There is no smile, nor hug – it will be a purely commercial session. I go to the bathroom. Although the uniform was the biggest available, it is quite an effort to squeeze into. I just manage to do up the buttons; however it is extremely short, hardly covering my thighs. I put my hair in bunches and cover my lips with pink lipstick, then go upstairs.

'I like that it is so short on your legs,' he states dispassionately. 'Get on the floor on your hands and knees, footstool.'

He watches TV, smokes, and sends me on a half-gin half-tonic errand every ten minutes. He makes me lick his shoes, crawl on the floor and fetch a wooden spoon from the kitchen.

'Bend over my knees.'

He lifts up my skirt.

'Where are the proper school panties? Have I not asked you to buy them?' he shouts.

I try and fish for an excuse, not having a clue what 'proper school panties' even are – and being too embarrassed to ask the shop assistants.

'Yes, you have – but ... I didn't find any in the store. They are all out of stock.'

He doesn't look convinced.

'Worthless piece of shit. You deserve nothing. You are not punctual, you haven't bought proper school panties, you don't obey the rules I set you. But you'll be put in your place tonight,' he says, hitting me with the wooden spoon.

'Get back on the floor under my legs, you useless footstool. Lift up your skirt.'

'Can I tell you something?' I ask him, from my position on the carpet.

'Shut up!' He's glued to the screen, drinking and smoking while resting his feet on my back. Eventually he allows me to move to the edge of the sofa and kneel at his feet.

'Now you can talk.'

'I just want to say I was so upset when you told me you were increasing commitments with your girlfriend. I got depressed, couldn't eat, just vomited everything out. I miss you, Daddy. I miss your cuddles and —'

His response is a big slap in the face.

There is an abrupt silence; he watches as the tears roll down my cheeks. He sticks his finger into my mouth. Automatically I start sucking it while he moves it around slowly, pushing it in and out, the salty taste of my tears all over it.

He asks me to bend over his knees and begins hitting me vigorously with the wooden spoon, making rapid

On Undefended Flesh

movements which become more and more aggressive – until I hear something snap.

'I've broken the wooden spoon on my little girl. I can't believe it.' He looks delighted as he holds the pieces up for me to see, then caresses my face gently. 'We should put it aside as a memory,' he says, smiling. 'But now let's go upstairs. I have to cane you.'

I bend over the pillows on the bed and he begins caning me. It hurts much more than the wooden spoon but I do my best to keep still and quiet. Soon the tormenting pain becomes too much, however, and I have to get up from the bed, unable to withstand it any longer. I'm crying, feeling my bruised thighs, when all of a sudden I become hysterical:

'That's my blood!' I scream, terrified by the sight of it all over my hands and the duvet. 'You beat me so hard that I'm bleeding!'

'Yes, you're bleeding,' he says calmly, reacting as though it was completely natural.

He walks me to the bathroom, sits on the bathtub and proceeds to clean the blood from my thighs; I lean against the sink, gazing at the sad, exhausted face in the mirror, the red mark across my cheek still glowing from his cruel slap. When he has finished he asks me to get on the floor. I do so robotically, and before I have time to wonder why, he starts kicking me.

He goes back to the bedroom. I pick myself up from

the tiles wearily to follow him.

'Stay on the floor. We haven't finished the caning, as you moved.'

I want to scream out. I've already suffered so much this evening. *It's too much!*

'You'll get three more strokes.'

When the first stroke comes it is so vicious I collapse back to the floor, screaming like mad. He aims his second one as I move away; it catches me on my belly, causing a large bleeding tear on my skin.

'I didn't mean to hit your stomach but you moved away,' he says, looking a little shocked.

He canes me softly for my final stroke, then starts rubbing his penis as I clean the blood off me. With the sight of my bruised and bloodied body it is not long before he ejaculates his sticky stuff.

After he has wiped himself dry and had a rest on the bed, we go back to the living room and chat.

'Where is she?'

'She's out on a bonding session for work. She's away quite often.'

'When will she be back?

'She'll be back after ten.'

'And what will she think when she sees the blood all over the duvet.'

'I'll tell her I've cut myself with the razor,' he says confidently, looking relaxed.

'Will she believe it?'

'What else can she do?' He shrugs his shoulders.

'You've caused a really nice mark on my stomach. See!' I show him my belly.

'Yes, it's lovely. Do you like it?'

'Yes, because it's from my Daddy.'

He smiles and pulls me towards him, wrapping me tight around his arms.

'Do you still find me intriguing?' I ask him.

'Yes. And I have to say that I'm more intrigued by you than ever. A large part of my mind is thinking about you. I just need time to decide what I should do.'

'How much time do you need?'

'Don't push me with time limits. Anyway, it's time for you to go home. It's nearly ten, the Spaniard will be home soon.'

I go to the bathroom and dress into my normal clothes, thinking of his words. He might say I occupy 'a large part' of his mind, but it's not me who's sharing his life. I notice a hole in my white socks and take it as bad omen: I have lost my Daddy, this may even be our last session together. Just like the wooden spoon, my heart is broken and seems impossible to fix.

He says goodbye to me at the front door with a reserved, passionless hug.

*

The following day I text him, hoping to flame his

interest.

/Little girl is so proud of the red stripe on her stomach. How does my Daddy feel about his little girl's severe beating yesterday?/

/Daddy enjoyed giving his little girl the punishment she deserved so much./

/You need to buy a new set of wooden spoons to break on your little girl. I can't wait to receive my next punishment./

/Did you like Daddy breaking a wooden spoon on your naughty bottom? How much punishment do you crave?/

/Little girl knows she deserves to be beaten. I enjoy every moment I spend with Daddy. I'd like to move further, but since you increased commitments with Spaniard everything has changed. What are your plans with your little girl?/

/Going to bed. Text you in a couple of days./

'Going to bed'? Probably cuddling his girlfriend right now. It's clear he wants to settle down with his girlfriend;

but I want him to want me, to beg for me. I would like to make him jealous, reject him and make him suffer like he does to me.

I check the replies from my posting on the Internet. There are many responses, but one in particular I find interesting:

> *If you are into having a dominant man and maybe a dominant 26-year-old girl cane you while you are bent over the back of a chair - whip you while you are hung in the hallway dressed like a servant - tell you to wash our clothes — by hand - tell you to stand up in the back of the bus — tied up - humiliate you in public (such as being taken out to a hot London restaurant with us - food arrives - you are told not to eat while we eat - food sits in front of you as everyone looks on - maybe getting on the floor of the bathroom to lick shoes for your dinner) - then you have found it. If not - delete this and move on. Want more ideas? Let's chat first. Email me now and we'll go from there.*
> *Mick@*

Intrigued by his idea of being humiliated in public, I reply to his message and receive a text the following morning.

/Are you still interested in being punished - humiliated - whipped into submission by a

Mick's Bitch

cruel master? Mick./

/Am interested. But you do know that I am commercial. Tell me about yourself, your requirements and expectations, please./

/Work near Liverpool Street Station - live in Earl's Court. I'm 40 - good-looking. Have had lots of experience in making a young woman a total submissive - humiliating her - whipping her till she begs and begs. You will love every minute of it as your body and soul is trodden on. I know you are commercial - that's fine./

/Sounds great. I could meet you today?/

/South Kensington tube - 6pm. We can meet for an interview to discuss the terms - how - when etc./

*

The bus terminates at the station.

/Come out the side - towards the Bank of Ireland sign across the road - turn right. Hold your phone to your ear. Black coat - tan pants./

He looks really confident and domineering – not too tall (around my height), bald, average build, with an arrogant voice. In his text he said he was forty, but he seems at least ten years older. He hails a cab and does not say a word to me during the trip, busily talking on his phone while directing the driver.

When we arrive at his apartment, he takes me straight into the living room and forces me to my knees. He's standing there in front of me, looking cruel and frightening, staring with fierce eyes. I begin to feel extremely vulnerable, uncomfortable and scared.

'You'll become my bitch.' He gives me a slap on the face, then another one. And he proceeds to beat me with his belt, which hurts terribly since my thighs are still sore from my last session in Chelsea.

'But I thought this was just an interview for you to test my submissive skills,' I say, after several straps.

'Yes, it's a test. Shut up, bitch!'

'But I can't take a severe beating now, my body is full of scars from my last session. Look!'

I can see the astonishment in his eyes as I pull down my jeans to reveal the markings on my skin. He seems quite convinced of my submissive abilities now, and gets me to crawl on the floor and lick his shoes. Then, with his belt fastened around my neck, he leads me to the kitchen like a dog and asks me to lick the tiles clean and shiny. Obediently I follow his command, but with considerable difficulty as he pulls the belt tighter.

Mick's Bitch

He leads me back to the spacious living room and begins stepping on my hands. It's terribly painful as he shifts his weight from his toes to his ankles, concentrating the pressure on my small fingers. Aware of how important first impressions are to experienced masters, I try to remain as silent as possible.

'Now, I'm going to turn you into the perfect bitch for us to play with.'

He leaves the room and comes back with a black top and miniskirt in his hands, asking me to change into them.

'That's great. You'll be a perfect bitch in that outfit,' he says, after I have changed.

Sitting casually in an armchair, he begins instructing me on how to move and pose, and how to use my body language.

'We can't go out for a public humiliation tonight because I have to go to a meeting. But next time you'll come as my bitch, dressed like this, all black … Move your right leg forward, left one back. That's it. Turn your head towards me.' He comes up to me and touches me on the bottom.

'I'll approach you in the bar and touch you so everyone can see you belong to me.' He laughs. 'You'll smile, showing that you enjoy my hands touching your arse in public.

'Also, you'll have to go flirt with the ugliest men in the bar. And when they ask you for a drink, you must tell them that you are not allowed since you are a slave who belongs to a master. Then you'll send them to my table, telling them that they must speak to your owner first if they want to get permission to use you.'

'But I've never flirted with men. And they won't be interested in me.'

'We'll see. I'm sure if they see you dressed like that they'll approach you. But you have to tell them that you are dedicated to me, that you're my little slut.'

I am nodding my head obediently.

'Now sit down. I'll teach you how to sit so that everyone can see your underwear ... Cross your legs. Right. Now lift up your right leg ... more! ... Lift it up properly! OK, that's enough. Excellent! So you have to sit in the bar exactly like that,' he says, laughing.

I'm not sure if I would be able to act like a real slut in public, trying to attract men in such a provocative way, but it would be interesting to find out; also, the lesson on how to use my body language has been quite informative. He starts chatting more casually now, and I find out a little more about him: he's a divorced South African merchant banker (which explains why I have trouble understanding his tricky accent) who has three girlfriends (another bastard who cheats!), all of whom are younger than his daughter.

'So I'll see you when you've healed and you'll then be really humiliated. I'll be away for a few weeks but I'll let you know when I get back.'

Mick's Bitch

He pays me forty pounds before I leave.

I awake the next morning to receive my daily text from Pete:

> /Shana! Can't keep texting and no reply. Do you want to fix a new date? I'm not short of contacts and it's hard getting anything fixed up with you./

… and also some from Mick:

> /You are now my bitch and submissive slave. Be prepared to be beaten. You are nothing./
> /Are you ready to be beaten and humiliated soon, BITCH? I will send you an email with some very bizarre things I am going to have you do. You will love it. My bitch./

> /I'm a bit concerned about my new role as I've never played a bitch. Being an innocent little girl is more comfortable and natural for me./

> /We will start as little girl - then work you into MY BITCH after time. You will not remember anything except that YOU ARE MY BITCH - doing what I say. You like it - don't

> you - being known as MICK'S BITCH./

… but *nothing* from Daddy.

> /Where is my Daddy?/
> /Little girl misses her Daddy so much./
> /Why don't you text your little girl? You promised to text me in a couple of days./

Eventually, later in the day, he responds.

> /Can't text now. I'm at work. Too many texts. Bit obsessive. Will text tonight./

'Obsessive'? I know he's right … it's ridiculous that I chase him with my texts. To an outsider it must appear that I am some crazed psycho. But I'm just an unlucky girl who fell in love with her Daddy, who was stringing her along, playing with her heart. The new texts from Pete can do nothing to distract me:

> /Can you do Thursday 23rd, Shana? Like to see you and it would be a fair session for a large fee. I could see you several times in next 2 months. Spanking only, as always – no sex interest./
> /And if I buy you a coffee or drink, it's still client/sub, nothing else, so relax. We are

**allowed to meet and discuss next meeting
arrangements. All right?/
/So send me just one text. Do you want me to
spank you in two weeks time? It's a long wait
but I'll do it if I'm sure you will meet me. We
can be spankee/client and still be friendly.
I like you – but not in any sex way. Just as a
nice girl./**

He's pathetic; yet the way he texts and begs for my attention is exactly how I behave with my Chelsea Daddy. But my Daddy ignores me – and as though in revenge, I do the same with Pete.

*

**/Little girl should report to her Daddy
7.30pm this Thursday for her severe
punishment./**

His text is sent on Sunday night, and although I'm aware it's only commercial, I'm looking forward to it immensely, just so I can spend time with him.

But on Wednesday I receive the bad news:

**/Tomorrow night is off. Change of plans. I
have kids again./**

I cannot believe it – I feel like I will explode. *He's making a fool of me again!*

>/It is the last time you make a fool of me.
>You'll never see me again. I won't be your
>little girl any more. Good luck with finding a
>new one. Goodbye./

He's only messing me around. I run to the store to pick up some groceries – rolls, cheese, milk, my usual stuff; I just want to get home quickly and cry out all my sorrows. In the queue I check my phone ... *nothing!* I was sure he'd respond to my dramatic announcement. It only makes me more desperate ...

>/I'm your loving little girl and I want to
>ask my Daddy to give me a time and a place
>tomorrow to meet ten minutes for a drink.
>Call or text me to discuss it./

A couple of hours later I realise my phone has been in voicemail mode. I'm trying frantically to return it to its usual settings, just in case he calls ... There's a new voice message. I calm myself down and listen to the familiar voice:

'Hi, it's your Daddy. Call me if you can in the next half hour or text me.'

I save the message straight away, the operator telling me it will be saved for three days. I replay it. Though it begins with a harsh cough, his voice sounds so nice and soft.

And now his text:

/Covent Garden tube tomorrow. 3pm./

I confirm the appointment.

Lying there in bed, I listen over and over to his message ... *'Hi, it's your Daddy. Call me if you can in the next half hour or text me. Bye'* ... like a soothing lullaby before sleep.

*

Much of the morning is spent preparing myself to look as good as I can. I put on my stretched black trousers that show my thighs and a striped T-shirt which I think suits me. I look plain but nice, like a little girl. But that stupid ugly spot should not be there above my lip right now. Why is it there today when I am meeting my Daddy? ... I try and cover it with foundation, apply some mascara and lip balm (the basic light make-up for a young girl), and spray some perfume on my neck. I'm imagining cuddling him, giving him a big hug – even if he does not want to, I will get it somehow. All my thoughts and preparations are now concerned with those ten small minutes.

After a mix-up, we finally locate each other.

'Where were you? I was waiting for you at Coffee and

On Undefended Flesh

Kink,' he says, looking surprised and exhausted.

'But you texted me the tube station.'

'Oh, you're right. It must have slipped my mind.'

'Shall I carry your bag? I ask him, while we are walking down the street.

'No, you don't have to,' he says. He seems very absent-minded.

'Are you busy at work?'

'Yes. You got me in a busy period. Sometimes there's not much to do, sometimes there's a lot, like now.'

We go to a small, hidden pub that is nearly empty. Buying a lager for himself and a mineral water for me, he brings them to the table.

'Such a surprise. The first time you are serving me. It should be the other way round.'

'That's true,' he says, and for the first time today I see him smile.

'Why don't you sit down?'

'No. I never sit down if I'm with a woman. It's a custom.'

I can't believe my ears. When I am at his place he puts his feet on me and beats me black and blue, and now he is concerned with gentlemanly manners.

'Why are you drinking alcohol if you are going back to work?'

'I always drink, even while at work.'

'And you don't get drunk?'

'No, I'm quite used to it,' he says casually.

Mick's Bitch

'I was so upset yesterday when you cancelled our session.'

'But we'll meet soon. Tomorrow, I'll text you which day. An overnight session, either Sunday or Monday. We'll have many opportunities since she studies away at university.'

'So you'll have more time for your little girl?'

'Yes, much more than before. Certainly the weekends.'

I feel delighted to hear the good news.

'But listen, I've got to get back to work now. I'll let you know tomorrow.'

'Can I give you a hug?' I ask him, when we are outside.

'Yes, but not here. It's too public.'

I lead him to a quiet, hidden space between two buildings, and wrap my arms around him tight.

'Just make it short,' he says, his face and body all rigid.

*

Saturday I receive his text:

> /Sunday or Monday evening 8-11pm. If you bring uniform Daddy will touch you up and molest you. Blow job first, maybe rape next. Daddy is going to severely punish you for your insolence./

On Undefended Flesh

That's not fair!

/You promised an overnight session, and now you give me only three hours! I'm going to visit you on both days, Sunday and Monday, even if you don't want it, because I want to spend more time with you./

/Right now get one thing clear: you do not turn up without an appointment. I may have kids staying. By all night I meant all evening. Unless you understand the appointment rule I won't see you tomorrow or ever again.
Confirm, please./

I feel devastated when I read this. These words are too harsh – 'get one thing clear', 'appointment rule', 'ever again'.

He calls me:

'I'm really upset by the text you sent me, saying that you would just turn up without an appointment.'

'Sorry, I didn't actually mean it. And I've never done that before.'

'Then why are you threatening that you will? Last time I said seven but you came at six. If people are just hanging around outside my house I may have to call the police.'

Mick's Bitch

'What are you talking about? I've never threatened you with the police, though I'm the one that could!' I burst out crying. 'And now you come out with that ... *that's not nice of you!*' I scream down the phone, losing all self-control.

'No, I don't want to call the police. But you can't just turn up whenever. I may have kids, guests ... '

'Do you want the session at all tomorrow?'

'I don't know.'

'You've really changed a lot. You only want to settle down, don't even seem keen to beat me.'

'Maybe.'

'So, I'm right. You've lost your kink?'

'Well, I don't seem as interested in caning, spanking and those other things. I'm not even keen on the videos.'

'What about your relationship with the Spaniard?'

'It's going quite well. I just want to give it a chance and see how it goes.'

'Can I at least visit you tomorrow evening for a chat?'

'OK, that's fine. Tomorrow.'

*

Sunday evening I visit. I had planned on leaving some 'female stuff' by accident during our session – lipstick on the bedside table, bottle of mascara under the bed or stockings in the bathroom. I wanted to make her jealous.

But now, there doesn't seem to be any point.

'So how are you getting on with your girlfriend?' I ask him in the living room.

'Well, we had a row. She asked me to stop drinking and smoking, and I asked her to lose weight.'

'And have you reached any consensus?'

'Yes, I'm going to cut cigarettes, and maybe alcohol ... no, I think I'll keep the spirits. But I want to reduce the cigarettes because I know I smoke too much.'

'And what about her? Is she going to lose weight?'

'I'll send her for liposuction, I think. At least that problem will be sorted.'

'Is that the only problem with her, that she's a bit overweight?'

'Yes, and also her English. I have to repeat myself all the time, because she has trouble understanding. It's a bit irritating.'

'What about you and me? Have you ever fancied me?'

'No, never. I contacted you only for the service you mentioned on your advert. But I don't want to talk about it.'

'So is there any space in your life for me?'

'No, none. I've got other issues that I want to concentrate on.'

'Will you ever contact me again if you get your kink back?'

'Yes, but last time it was ten years that I wasn't

interested in it. It's been like that – on and off – most of my life.'

I'm sitting there, completely despondent.

'There's one thing you need to do for me urgently. You must delete all the text messages I sent you on your phone.'

'Why?'

'Because you visit many different clients and you may get involved in very dangerous sessions with real weirdos. I don't want to be blackmailed by anyone.'

'Do you think I'd ever be able to blackmail you?' I ask, offended.

'No, I'm not talking about you, I'd never think of you as being someone like that. But you may have clients who could threaten me in some way. It's very important, and I trust that you'll delete them as soon as you get home. Will you?' He gives me a very serious look.

'Yes, I will,' I confirm, despite the fact that I know I will not.

He leads me to the front door.

'Will I see you again?' I ask, before leaving.

'Maybe yes, maybe no,' he says with a wry grin. And he gives me a kiss on the hand like this is farewell for ever.

12

Trick or Treat

I'm on the bus going home. It's the 31st of October – *Halloween* – and I can see groups of children on the streets, dressed in their scary outfits, ready to begin their 'trick or treat' mission. Though it's only five-thirty, it's already dark, the clocks having been turned back an hour last week; winter is coming, and every day is getting a little colder and darker. I've just completed the early shift at work and am returning to my box – tired, hungry and lonely.

When I arrive home I head straight for my mattress and stare at the ceiling. It's been over two weeks and I know I shouldn't – in case it's too obsessive – but if he sends me a reply I will get a tiny portion of happiness

Trick or Treat

and sleep well tonight; if not, I will carry on torturing myself, thinking about him. I grab for the phone.

/Little girl is missing her Daddy and his severe punishments./

/Daddy will pull your school panties down and inspect your pussy, then insert two, three, four fingers. You will cry and I will put whole fist in. You will then get 200 strokes./

/That sounds amazing, like a film. We could make our own home movie. What title would you like to give it?/

/Blood Soaked Daughter./

I repeat the words softly, imagining the bloody scenes, imagining my own horror movie. I finish my dinner and am ready to go to sleep when I receive an unexpected phone call.

'Hi, it's your Daddy. Is that little girl?'
'Yes, it's your little girl.'
'How are you?'
'I'm fine. I'm so happy that I can hear your voice. I'm so delighted you called.'

I'm so shocked that he called. He never does, unless

there is a big reason. What could he want?

'Have you ordered the DVDs?' (I see, the movies. He's so obsessed by them.)

'You said last time you've lost your kink. So why do you want spanking movies?'

'I might get the kink back if I receive a nice collection of perverted movies.'

'You know October has just gone and this is the first month that you didn't punish me since we met.'

'Do you miss your Daddy?'

'I miss you a lot. The sessions were such a memorable experience.'

'Why?'

'I don't know. It was so exciting – preparing myself for the sessions, having something to look forward to, buying uniforms, getting dressed to look pretty for Daddy. It was all so amazing.'

'Then why don't you come over?'

'When?'

'Now.'

He must be drunk or his girlfriend must be away and he is bored, otherwise he would not invite me. I should show him that I am strong, that I refuse to be his toy … but like usual I am weak.

'Are you sure? It's late.' I pretend to be reluctant, though I would run to him at any hour.

'Yes, come over now. Why not?'

'But it will take me an hour to get ready and go

there.'
'That's fine.'
'Shall I bring my uniform?'
'Yes, bring it with you. See you soon.'
'See you, Daddy.'

I lie there bewitched for a few minutes … until I jump up from the bed; I need to take a shower, not to mention shave my awfully hairy legs – and my pussy, of course, for him. I try to be as quick as possible, knowing the faster I am the sooner I can be with my Daddy. The fact that I arrived home dead tired is swiftly forgotten. Now I'm not sleepy at all – on the contrary, I am full of energy. Such a surprise, such a treat. Hopefully it turns out to be a treat rather than a trick.

It's ten o'clock. I'm running to the bus stop, so happy to be catching number 137 – my favourite bus. I get off at Chelsea and start walking along King's Road, checking my appearance in the large shop windows … not my best, but hopefully he won't notice in the dim light which he always favours.

It's already late by the time I ring the bell.

'It's me,' I say into the speaker.

I open the door and leave my uniform and shoes in the hall. I'm a little confused as he does not come down to greet me, but he soon calls for me from upstairs.

'Where are you?' I respond.

'I'm already in bed,' he yells from above.

On Undefended Flesh

I make my way up to the room. He's in bed looking a little strange, absent-minded, probably drunk.

'Come here.'

I crawl to him on my knees and rest my head on his tummy and start cuddling him.

'My Daddy.'

'Take off your clothes,' he says.

I remove my T-shirt.

'I feel more comfortable in my school uniform,' I say, not keen on the thought of being naked straight after my arrival.

'Then go and put on your uniform.'

That would be better. I run downstairs to change into my white blouse, white socks and grey tunic. Then I return to him, placing myself in the same position – on my knees, my head in his lap, my bottom exposed provocatively to attract his attention to spank me – but he does not; instead, he takes his penis and starts stroking my bare bottom with his other hand.

'Touch Daddy's penis.'

I know I should not be doing it, shouldn't be obeying a man who constantly breaks my heart, but he takes my strength and dignity whenever I am with him. I start to rub it, while he touches my thighs gently.

'Put it into your mouth,' he asks me softly.

'No, I can't.'

I always found the idea of blow jobs disgusting, and decided I would never do it for anyone, not even someone

I loved. If someone loved me they would not ask me to do something that I do not feel comfortable doing.

He tries to force me by pushing my head towards it, but I move away.

'You have to put it into your mouth, if you want your Daddy.' He looks at me strictly but I do not fall for his blackmail.

He hands me an empty glass.

'Go to the kitchen and bring me half Scotch and half water.'

He already seems tipsy and he wants more ... *I will give him more!* I like it when he's drunk since he is more gentle and says nice things that he wouldn't normally say.

As I'm leaving the room he asks me to lift up my skirt. When I look back I see his dissatisfied expression.

'What's wrong?' I ask, surprised; my skin is all pure and I have not had a session in ages.

'The panties,' he shouts angrily. 'You're not wearing proper school panties.'

'But I didn't know you'd call me tonight. I didn't have time to buy them,' I reply.

I run to the kitchen and prepare his drink, measuring a tiny amount in soda water and the rest in whisky.

As I place the glass on the bedside table, he invites me into his bed and starts cuddling me. He's holding me so tight and it feels so good.

'We should stop this commercial relationship and

switch to something more emotional.'

I stare at him, astonished.

'Oh, what am I saying?' He puts his hand to his forehead and starts rubbing it.

'I'd be happy to quit the commercial line and am willing to be beaten for free,' I say. Now I am just as astonished by my own words: since becoming a submissive, to receive some kind of financial reward for pain has always been an important principle of mine – but I'm willing to give it up, if it means I can have him.

'Well, I would pay you say two hundred pounds per week because I have to reimburse you in some way.'

'I'm so happy you got back to me. I missed you so much.' I move closer to him. 'I thought I would lose you forever.'

'You almost did.'

'When?'

'When we were to go to the seaside.'

'But it was your fault since you promised to take me for an Aston Martin drive and then you became so funny and sent me home.'

'Yes, I know. Can you remember how weird I was?'

'But I don't want to lose my Daddy again. I want to be your non-commercial little girl.'

He looks at me. His face is all nice and friendly as he pulls me towards him.

'I like being with you. I like spending time with you. I like you a lot,' he says gently.

I'm lying on his chest holding him very tight, bathing in the joy of those words. I feel so high. Maybe we really can start a purely emotional relationship. But the germ of doubt surfaces to my mind. He's let me down before. What about the Spaniard, have they had a fight? When he is sober what will he think then?

'Where is she?' I ask, needing to know.

'She's away.'

'But what has happened with you and her?'

'Claudia?' He sighs and his voice becomes sad. 'I don't want to talk about her.'

For the first time I hear her name and I'm taken aback; it sounds much more personal than 'the Spaniard'. Doubt floods my mind. Deep in my heart I know I should not be here. But it feels so pleasurable, so secure; I want to believe that it is all true.

'OK, then we won't talk about her. So what will I be for you? Your little girl, your lover, or what?'

He turns to me and says softly, 'You'll be my little girl and I'll be your Daddy. Daddy will adopt you. You'll be my worthless adopted daughter.'

'We should spend more time to get to know each other.'

'Yes, we'll spend lots of time together. We'll go to the seaside in the Aston Martin.'

'I love you, Daddy. I love you so much.' I wrap my hands around his neck and start kissing his face.

'But you can't say "I love you." You mustn't become

emotional.'

'What about "I like you"? Can I say that?'

'Well — yes — you can,' he says, hesitating before giving permission. 'Just hanging around, having fun. No emotional outbursts, no going bonkers and we'll see how it goes.'

'Sounds great. Hanging out with Daddy. We'll have lots of fun, spending more time together. I'll be your naughty little girl.'

'My naughty little girl.' He smiles and hugs me gently.

'So it won't be all about caning, beating and humiliation.'

'No, that will be just one part.'

'And can we go on without having sex?'

'No. Daddy will finger you and rape you soon.'

'Would you like it?'

'Yes, Daddy would love to molest his little girl regularly.' He's getting turned on and begins rubbing his penis while holding me tight in his other arm. 'How old will you be when Daddy rapes you?'

'How old do you want me to be?'

'Eleven.' He begins rubbing his penis vigorously.

An eleven-year-old girl,' I say absent-mindedly.

'Touch Daddy's penis now.'

I hold it in my hand, moving it up and down.

'Show me your breasts.'

I start unbuttoning my white shirt but it's difficult

with only one hand. He becomes impatient and rips a button off. He cannot wait to feel my small tits ... those tits that help him imagine he really is with a little girl.

'Suck my penis.'

I look at him.

'Suck your Daddy's penis. Be a good girl.' He is caressing my hair gently and pushing my head towards it, trying to make me do what I do not want to do.

'Just kiss it. Kiss Daddy's penis.'

Maybe if I touch it with my lips he will love me more. I should put it into my mouth; it cannot be that disgusting because I love him so much. I love my Daddy. I would do anything for him – almost anything – but I'm not sure about his feelings. He just uses me for his own pleasure, messes me around all the time. No, I won't suck it, I need to be sure about his feelings ... But I am so close to it.

I kiss the peak of it.

'Kiss it again,' he encourages me.

I keep on kissing it, realising it is not as horrible as I imagined. Though it is far from the oral satisfaction he probably desired, it is one step further that I have taken. I look at him waiting for a rewarding smile but his expression is stony. He pulls my panties down and puts his fingers into me, giving me the so-called fingering that he has always promised me. I can feel his index and middle fingers moving inside my pussy. His movements are not gentle and are deliberately violent to cause me pain. A weak sorrowful scream leaves my mouth; it hurts and I'm concerned about losing my virginity in such a senseless way.

He turns over and lies on the bed, still rubbing his penis. I rest my head on his chest.

'I'll always be beside you, whenever you need some company, pleasure, joy. I'll be your caring little girl. I love – sorry – *like* my Daddy very much.'

He starts sighing heavily …

After he wipes himself clean, he takes me into his arms and begins talking about a completely different subject:

'I've always been asked by journalists to give interviews, a personal profile to business columns, but I've always rejected those offers.'

'Why? It could be beneficial for your business.'

'Yes, I know, but I don't want to be in the spotlight. I've never longed for publicity, and still they ask me to tell them how I've made my fortune. Lately they interviewed this gay guy that I know, asking him how he earned his million. But that's ridiculous – one million pounds is nothing!'

Maybe for him! Though I've always been curious as to how much money he really has, I never dared to ask.

'But I recently gave an interview with a newspaper last week.'

'Really? I'm so proud of you, Daddy. When will it appear?' I ask, caressing him gently.

'In a few weeks.'

'I don't understand why you're so reluctant about publicity. You're such a great person.'

'Everyone knows I'm fantastic. There's no need for articles,' he says with a grin.

'You're a fantastic Daddy, a fantastic businessman, a great man.'

'I'm just an English eccentric really. Like James Bond.'

'Well, you've got the Aston Martin, you're charming and good-looking. You're my James Bond.'

'Yes, I've got the car. It's amazing when I drive it and hear that engine. Such a shame that it sits there in the garage.'

'Do you like living here?' I ask him.

'I love this house. I'd say it's the best place to live in London.'

'That's quite a strong statement.'

'It is. But listen ... just be quiet ...' We are lying there on the bed listening to the faint distant noises from outside. 'It's so quiet. No police cars, no fire brigades —'

'Only if Daddy starts cooking.'

He laughs at my reference to an incident in the summer he had told me about: he had been so busy cooking one evening that he didn't notice all the smoke coming out of his kitchen until the firemen showed up.

'It's a wonderful house, a great place to live. And it's close to everything.'

On Undefended Flesh

He turns to me all bright and excited.

'You said you didn't want to appear in _____ Movies because you're concerned it may be embarrassing later in your life.'

'That's right.'

'I don't think you should worry about it. It's not going to go out to the wider public. You should go for it. It would be great.'

'I don't know,' I say, hesitating, surprised by his enthusiasm.

'I'd like to be there. I could book a flight for both of us for a weekend away. You'd be doing the film and I'd be there in the background as an outsider.'

'Maybe. And what about the spanking website? Should I advertise myself there?'

'No. I've told you it's too dangerous. There are so many weird men.'

He says it so caringly, as though he were my real dad. He doesn't want me to get into any dangerous situations, but he wants me to appear in a brutal spanking movie where I'll be beaten black and blue. *Such a loving Daddy ...*

'Next year I'm turning twenty-five. It's terrible,' I sigh sadly.

'It is terrible indeed. Terribly old,' he says, smiling.

'And you'll be forty-nine.'

'It doesn't matter how old I am,' he says wryly.

'Kiss me, Daddy.'

Trick or Treat

He never wants to kiss me, and this time his kiss is no different: weak, without passion or emotion. Suddenly he slaps me in the face. He's looking at me, his face above mine, all strict and severe.

'What do you have to say?'

I'm lying there, confused.

'Thank you, Daddy ... May I have another one?'

He gives me another one, and repeats it again and again, slapping me until I feel I will lose some teeth. I start crying and he stops to cuddle me. He then asks me to expose my bare bottom, and he sticks his fingers into my arse. I start whining but he carries on; it's painful and in a strange way it really does feel like I am being molested by my daddy.

With his free hand he continues to touch himself, rubbing it for a while, but the sticky stuff won't come out. Instead he checks his phone, then makes a call. It goes to voicemail so he begins to text.

'Who are you texting?' I ask him suspiciously, worried that it may be the Spaniard.

'My daughter is at a concert with her friend. Her friend's mother is to pick them up, but I don't know when she'll be back. I'm quite a neurotic father.'

'You're such a daddy.' I smile back at him.

Finally he manages to reach her on the phone.

'Hi, Jessica. Where are you? Is everything all right?' His voice is so gentle, full of love and concern. 'What was the concert like? ... Oh, that's great ... How will you get back? ... All right ... I'll let you in. Just ring the bell ... No, don't worry. I'll be up ... See you soon. Bye.'

Every word he uses, the intonation of his voice, reveals how devoted he is to his kids. He really must be a gorgeous daddy.

'Is she coming home?'

'Yes, she'll be here in fifteen minutes.'

'So I have to go home?'

'I assumed you'd stay overnight.'

'But your daughter is coming.'

'Don't worry. She and her friend will be staying downstairs.'

I'm delighted and surprised he would let me stay. But I am also worried: my emotions grow stronger the longer I am with him – if he lets me down later it will only hurt more.

When she arrives he goes down to greet her. After he returns he quickly falls asleep. He looks so sweet; I kiss his face, his eyes, his hair. I adore him and am overwhelmed I can be here ... yet I do not feel secure; when the morning comes and he is sober, will my joy be drowned by tears?

It's cold in the room so I get up to close the window. The glass of whisky is still there, almost full, on the bedside table. He was planning on finishing it and having a cigarette but his attempt was defeated by the fairy of dreams. I watch him: he has a big smile across his face.

Trick or Treat

What could he be dreaming about? I just hope it is not the Spaniard.

I cover him with the duvet and go to the bathroom. Sitting on the toilet, I notice some red patches on my white panties. I'm concerned – hopefully I haven't lost my virginity, I would regret it so much. There's not a huge amount of blood but I'm pretty sure it's not my period, and it doesn't look like that anyway. No, it's definitely from his fingers. Now I'm really ashamed that I let him do that. I try to calm myself, concluding the blood was caused by his fingers scratching me, and would not have affected my virginity; it would have been much more painful and there would have been more blood.

I gaze into the mirror ... I look OK, but sad – with slap marks across my face. Like an innocent little girl, I stand there in my school tunic, my long brown hair dangling over my white skin.

Inquisitive, I open a wardrobe. Her clothes are there among Daddy's suits; a red spotted shirt, a green dress, a brown cardigan. It angers me that they are there. I want to grab them and tear them into little pieces, blow my nose in them, pee on them ... or just hang my uniform next to them. I close the door and go back to bed, my confidence and faith in my Daddy diminishing.

It's 3 o'clock in the morning and still I am awake. I'm concerned about the morning. Will he cuddle me when he wakes? Will he call me his little girl? Or will he be completely sober and act different? I try to stay optimistic ...

He has been snoring and moving around the bed all night but I don't mind as long as I'm near him. Lying there, I continue to watch him in the moonlight; he looks so cute and vulnerable, like a little boy.

At half past six I awake. He's still sleeping, lying across the bed, taking up all the space. I'm so excited. I'd like to wake him up and cuddle him but I let him sleep. Hopefully when he does wake he will pull me into his arms like he used to. I check his alarm clock. It's set for seven but I change it to a few minutes earlier; I just can't wait to get my morning cuddle.

Finally he wakes, but does not pull me towards him. I try to initiate a conversation to break the ice.

'You were snoring all night. I only had a little space beside you since you kept turning as well.'

'I pushed you out?' he says, smiling.

He gets up and goes to the bathroom without as much as a glance my way.

'Why don't you cuddle your little girl?' I ask him, on his return.

'Daddy has to get ready for work.'

'But you used to cuddle your little girl in the morning.'

Ignoring me completely, he goes to the door and

listens carefully for any noise from downstairs. There mustn't be any, for he takes his belt and whips me – just once, he does not want to risk more. Then he takes his penis in his hands and asks me to kiss it and move it up and down, giving me a cold perfunctory cuddle for the sake of completing his duty to his little girl. I do what he asks and it is not long till he ejaculates, some of his sticky stuff falling on my tunic.

He seems so serious. Last night felt so promising, the beginning of our non-commercial relationship ... now it is all uncertain. I change out of my school uniform, but before getting dressed I go to the bathroom naked with the hope of turning him on. He is not impressed, however, and does not bother to look as he gets into the shower.

After he returns to the bedroom he starts getting dressed. While's he's sitting on the bed, putting on his socks, I begin to kiss his back. I catch the scent of his cologne.

'You smell nice.'

He does not say a word.

'Last night I noticed some blood on my underwear. What does it mean? I hope you didn't take my virginity.'

'No, I didn't. What are you talking about?'

'I was just scared when I saw the blood on my panties and I don't know why it was there. Do you have any idea?'

'I don't know, maybe some scratches.'

'If I lost my virginity there would have been much more blood. Am I right?'

'Yes, lots of blood.'

He continues with his dressing, ignoring me.

'You didn't tell me about her. What happened? Where is she?'

'I don't want to talk about it.'

'Do you feel guilty now?'

'No.'

'So that means your relationship is not going well. If it was, you would feel guilty.'

'Like I said, I don't want to talk about it. So stop it.'

But I need to know what is going on. Why can't he be straightforward? I am overcome with nostalgia as I think about how we used to have tea in bed together in the summer ... but now he won't even look at me.

He asks me to go home.

'Daddy, tell me what's going on, please. I need to know.' I wrap my arms around him.

'I'll tell you later. I'll call you.'

He gives me a quick wooden hug and leads me downstairs. He's very cautious, listening carefully so as to avoid any awkward encounter with his daughter. When we get to the bottom I realise I have left my uniform in his bedroom.

'Don't worry about it. I'll sort it out later.'

He wants to get rid of me as soon as possible. I also

Trick or Treat

find my purse empty — this is the first time I will not receive my pocket money.

'Can you give me some money for my bus fare?'

'Yes, of course, I just have to find my wallet.'

He goes upstairs and returns a few minutes later with my uniform.

'I can't find my wallet,' he says, and goes to look in the kitchen. It's unbelievable that a millionaire does not have ten pounds in his pocket, but I realise I will have just enough for a single ticket anyway and tell him not to worry.

He comes to the front door.

'Will you call me?' I ask, my eyes beseeching him.

'Of course. I'll call later this week.' He gives me an unconvincing smile before shutting the door.

13

Game Over, Daddy

/I am so happy that I can be your non-commercial little girl. It will be lots of fun./

By the following morning there is still no reply, so I call him.

'Why didn't you text me last night?'
'I went to bed early. I'm waiting for a taxi, going to Dublin now.'
'But when can we talk?'
'I'll call you on the weekend.'
'Will you? Definitely?'
'I will. Now I have to go. Bye.'
I calm down a bit. His voice was relaxed; he's probably

Game Over, Daddy

in business mode. I just need to be patient.

Another day goes by.

> /I got you back on Tuesday night and don't want to lose you again. Text your little girl./
> /What's going on? I need to know. Are you still in Dublin or already back in London?/

After another night with tearful eyes and confusion, I call him.
'You didn't text me back last night.'
'I was at a cocktail party. I've told you I'll call on the weekend. Now I've got to go to meetings.'
'Will you really call?'
'Yes, I will. When I get back.'
I try to reassure myself that he really is busy, that is why he cannot focus on me. At least while he is away he is not with the Spaniard.

Saturday morning. It's now been four days since that unexpected visit to his place. Finally he will contact me ... but I just can't wait:

> /How is my Daddy on this bright sunny Saturday morning? I'm so looking forward to hearing from you as you promised./

On Undefended Flesh

There is no reply after three long hours.

/Text me Daddy, please./

/Busy. Will text tomorrow./

/What are you busy with? When can you call me? Do you still want me to be your little girl?/

/Can't talk, with Spaniard. Maybe is all I'll say. Now please leave me alone. I'll text you tomorrow./

Having received his message while at work, I can no longer concentrate on my tasks, and simply go through the motions of placing shoes on and off customers' feet. The words *'leave me alone'* continue to play in my mind. On Tuesday he was cuddling *me*, saying how much he liked being with *me*, but now he is with *her*. They have reconciled and are happy: I have been made a fool of yet again.

At night I try to call, but he switches to voicemail. It makes me furious:

/I'm sure she's got other guys when she's away. She loves your money only. She'll leave

Game Over, Daddy

> you one day. No one can love you as much as I do./
> /I can offer you my youth, my virginity, my submission. I'm ready to be completely dedicated to you. I know you'll always get back to me because I am your little girl who loves you./

And the next morning:

> /Can I please visit you tonight after work around 9? We can chat./

> /Can't see you this evening. With Spaniard, then kids. I'll call you later. Leave me alone. I'll call./

At 8pm I finish work, then rush to the bus stop and switch on my mobile. Now finally I will hear the truth. I give him a miscall; he then phones.

'I can't talk now. I'm with the kids. I'll call you tomorrow.'

'I can't believe it. You promised me all week that you'd call me on the weekend. Yesterday you said you'd call me on Sunday and today you say you'll call me tomorrow. That's not fair.'

'I can't talk now.'

'Why don't you reply to my texts?'

'They're irritating.'

'But I need to know what's going on. Do you still want me?'

'I don't know. I'll call you tomorrow. Maybe is all I can say now.'

'But I'll be working tomorrow.'

'What time do you start work?'

'Eleven.'

'I'll call you before you start work.'

Bastard! Fake promises all the time. He does not care about me at all. He does not text me, does not call, always says tomorrow; I cannot wait to get home and burst into tears. Again, I am the fool – he is killing my soul, breaking my heart, destroying my self-esteem, ruining my emotions.

My desire for vengeance grows all night and threatens to take over ... *Little girl will be cruel and will not lose the game again. She will not let him make her feel miserable. She must be ruthless if they ever play with her heart.*

*

It's Monday morning. My heart is throbbing as though it were awaiting some pleasant news, even if I'm certain that it will soon feel only pain.

The phone is buzzing. The screen displays his name and number.

'Good morning, Mr _____ ,' I say, trying to be as formal as possible. (He has never told me his name,

Game Over, Daddy

I just stumbled across it on a document at his place; likewise, he has never asked for my real name – nor is he interested.)

'Good morning.'

A short silence follows, which is broken by me as I cannot wait to hear the truth.

'So tell me what's going on. You called me last Tuesday and said you like being with me and would like to move on to an emotional relationship together. Then you promised to call and text and you didn't. So?'

'Well, I do apologise for last Tuesday. The truth is that I was drunk, that's why I said those things that I should not have. Now I've sorted out things with my girlfriend and everything's fine.'

'So you're in love again?'

'Yes, we are.'

These words cut deeply. Although I was expecting this, why does it hurt excruciatingly?

'And what about me?'

'I want to be with my girlfriend and that's the way it is.'

'But you said I'm your little girl.'

'I live with someone else and I'm not going to talk about it any more. I'll go now. I'm going to the gym, I'm waiting for the car. So bye.'

NO! You will not get rid of me that easily. He is so arrogant, doesn't give a damn about my feelings. He cannot imagine how I suffer because of him. He lied to me last

Tuesday and now he thinks he can just throw me out like a disposable tissue.

'OK, then I'll sell the story to the tabloids. I've got all your text messages saved in my mobile and I've still got marks on my body. You'll be publicly embarrassed. It's going to be my sweet revenge. Bye.'

I do not wait for any reaction – just hang up. Now I have lost him for good, but I want him to know that he can't play with my heart. *He ruined my emotions so I will ruin his life.*

It must have worked for he immediately calls back. I let it keep ringing, then finally answer it.

'*Please, don't do it!* I have feelings towards you. You can text me any time. We can meet up if you want, you can be my little girl. *Please, please don't do it!*'

He sounds so pathetic and miserable as he begs. How ironic: he would rest his feet on my back, beat me black and blue, act all arrogant and confident, and now he is whining on the phone, begging for my mercy. His voice is so nervous I can hear his gasps for air. *So who is in control now?*

'I don't believe you and I don't trust you any more.'

'I'll meet you again. *Please!*'

'But I don't want to see you. I've had enough of you. Now everyone will know about your secret life.'

'Please, I have feelings for you. I'm just so confused. I get both hot and cold. Of course I want to see you again,' he exclaims anxiously.

Game Over, Daddy

'But I don't want you. Game over, Daddy. I can see the nice headlines: "Chief Exec Cuts Hungarian" or "Chief Executive's Perverted Dreams". What do you think?'

'Don't do it. Why do you want to destroy my children's lives?'

'No, I don't want to destroy their lives,' I reply, my nerve beginning to falter now that he has mentioned his kids. 'It's not their fault their Dad is a bastard. I hate you. But don't worry, I'll kill myself, I know this is what you want.'

'Don't be silly.'

'It will be a relief for you.' Losing all my strength, I start crying on the phone. 'You were the first and only man I loved. But you don't need me. I'm not even good enough for beating. I'm ugly, stupid, worthless – like you always say.'

'Don't tell me these silly things. There are plenty of things ahead of you.'

'No, I will kill myself. But before I do, I'll put you in hot water since you should suffer like me. You're a cruel bastard.'

'I'm just an Englishman,' he states.

'Don't tell me every English man is a bastard like you. I've met many nice, friendly, decent people here. You're conceited, selfish and cruel.'

'I don't think I am a bad person.'

'Well, you might be a wonderful father and you might be successful in your business, but your emotional life is a disaster.'

'Yes, that's true,' he says, his voice becoming soft and sad.

'Not only have you disappointed me, but you cheat on your girlfriends, you've been divorced.'

'Yes, I know I have a problem with relationships.'

'And you drink and smoke too much because you don't want to face reality.'

'Yes, my life is not complete,' he says, now sounding quite despondent.

'Why don't you marry your girlfriend, instead of keeping us guessing?'

'No, that's the last thing I want. It's more a relationship of convenience, there is no chemistry.' He pauses, I hear him swallow. 'I'll tell you something I've never told anyone. How many times do you think I have had sex with her in the past six months?'

'I don't know. Two or three times a week.'

'No. You'll be surprised, but I swear on my mother's life it happened only once in the last six months.'

I become lost for words. 'I thought you made love every time you met, and the spanking was just a kink you used to spice up your sex life.'

'No, not at all. Why do you think I need all those spanking videos?' he says, embarrassed.

'So what do you do in bed?'

'Well, we just sleep.'

'But does she not want it?'

'Yes, she wants it, but I'm not interested.'

'So why is she living with you at all?'

'I don't know. Sometimes I ask myself the same question.'

'But you had sex with the Australian in Japan this summer, and during our sessions you always had lots of sticky stuff.'

'Yes, I know.'

'So what's wrong?'

'I don't know, but I feel depressed.' He sounds quite upset now. 'Sorry, I'll call you back in a minute. I have to cancel the car, I'm not going to the gym.'

After he calls back he opens up to me further. He explains how his relationship with his kids has been blossoming of late and what a magical feeling that is; he talks about his failed marriage and how things started going wrong when he began making money; most of all, he speaks of the great unhappiness he feels and that he's living a life that does not make him feel whole.

The more we talk, the more my anger dissipates. The emotional strings I have attached to him are letting go as I realise the picture I have painted is very different to the reality: he is not a sagacious and mature man, but rather a lost boy.

Though this could be our last conversation together, I am feeling strangely delighted, not to mention *empowered*. To hear him beg like that, to know that at least for a moment I was more important to him than anything else — the gym, the office, whatever — felt so good. Who would have thought that a wealthy, esteemed Englishman's life could be destroyed by a 'worthless piece of shit', that the so-called *humil* in his phonebook could make him plead and gasp. Though I don't think I could have ever really carried out my threat (besides, would it be much of a sensational story at all, I wonder), for once he realised what it meant to feel vulnerable, knowing he might lose everything.

We've been on the phone for almost two hours before we finally say goodbye:

'I don't know what to say, I've never had such a conversation like this before with anyone. There's no one on this planet who knows more about me than you do now.'

'Then watch out, I can be dangerous for you,' I say.

He lets out a subdued laugh.

'Yes, you can.'

14

Public Humiliation

When I travel on business I expect you will text me. Whether I answer or not - I DON'T care.

This is a list of things you will have to look forward to when I get back:

1) Melanie and I will send you to our favourite bar. You will be in short skirt - all black - NO COAT - and stand outside in front of the window - while we drink in the warm bar.

2) Melanie is going to pour a glass of water down you - and send you back out in the cold - WET.

3) When we allow you inside - you will be told to sit at the bar - spread your legs - and show your black underwear to all - while we slap you in the face.

On Undefended Flesh

4) You will flirt with an ugly fat man at the bar - tell him you are a slave and need to get permission to talk to him. You will come over to us - get on your knees - and ask if you can talk to him. Melanie will slap you across the face - and send you back to talk.

5) You will tell him that you are 'owned' - and that if he wants to fuck you - you will have to get permission. You will NOT fuck him - but show him your black underwear - and tell him you can't.

6) You will fetch us a cab. You cannot sit on the seats - but on the floor - licking Melanie's high heels and the hem of her skirt.

7) When we get back to my place - Melanie will sit on your face - jumping up and down.

8) Since she weighs less - you will ride her around on your back - as I whip your arse with a wooden spoon.

9) We will sit you on a chair - tie your hands behind you - and slap your face many many many times.

10) You will take off your clothes and crawl around the floor - as we beat you with a belt - laughing at you.

11) Melanie will stand on your hands - while I beat you with anything from around the room.

12) You will be paid for this.

And there will be more - so text me and tell me if you still love your master.

Mick@

Public Humiliation

/One thing you will learn: when someone is in a SLAVE position at a public place - people like to see that - it excites them and makes their imagination run. People like to see someone being controlled. Most people really want to do this to someone - it is human nature - people like to 'control' someone at certain levels. Not all will go as far as we will - many never have the ability to actually follow through. Some will be shocked./
/So before I leave today - do you have any questions about Melanie and what the BOTH of us are going to do to you? We will not leave marks on your face since you have to go to work. But as for the rest of your body - too bad. And just remember: you're OUR BITCH./

*

The time for my public humiliation has finally arrived. I head out the door, head to toe in black, curious as to how the evening will unfold. How far will this bastard and his evil companion go? What will other people think of our bizarre behaviour – will they react at all?

My first challenge comes early: it's the first time I have worn high heels in public, and though it's dark and hardly anyone is about, those who are look bemused by my stumbling over the wet pavement. Conceding defeat, I return home, change into my comfortable black loafers

On Undefended Flesh

and place the high heels in my handbag, all the while recalling my grandmother's warning never to turn back if I forgot something as it would only bring bad luck.

It takes almost an hour for my bus to get to Bank Station, my destination. Mick calls me, trying to work out where I am, and we bump into each other around some statue.

'Follow me,' he says soberly, returning his mobile to his pocket.

He tells me that his first choice of venue – the bar – is closed, so he leads me to a posh restaurant instead, full of well-to-do people. The girl is already there, seated. We look at one another, but say nothing. (It feels rather awkward, but what should I say? 'Hi Melanie, nice to meet you. Let me introduce myself: I'm the bitch you're going to beat up tonight.' Keeping quiet seems more appropriate.)

Mick gives her a big hug, and they start chatting away, ignoring me in the process.

Quite some time passes before Mick turns to me.

'Can you see that woman in the purple top?' He points to an attractive woman alone at the bar. 'Go there. Stand next to her.'

'But why? What do you want me to do?'

'Just stand there. Smile, flirt with the men nearby.'

'But I don't know how,' I respond, my confidence already deserted.

Our conversation is interrupted by a waiter who takes

Public Humiliation

our drinks order. Mick and Melanie order champagne and mineral water. The waiter turns to me, but Mick steps in.

'Just ignore her. She doesn't want anything. *Am I right, bitch?*' He whispers the last words discreetly into my ear.

Again Mick tells me to go over to the woman, but I'm reluctant, the art of socialising having always been beyond me.

'I'd rather stand outside in the cold.'

'You want to stand outside?'

'Please.'

'OK. Stand up and go. We'll let you know when you can come back.'

I go outside. It is really cold, especially in my mini-skirt, and I resign myself to watching the smartly dressed people making their way home after a busy day in the City. Almost thirty minutes goes by before Melanie starts looking for me, but she neglects to check around the corner where I'm hiding. After hanging around looking perplexed, she returns inside. Waiting a few minutes, I follow.

'Melanie was looking for you,' Mick says, his eyes blazing furiously. 'Go to her now, she is in the toilet.'

Perhaps I will now have to wipe her bum as punishment. There is only one cubicle shut closed when I arrive; it must be her. I stand there uncertain whether to make my presence known. When she comes out she washes her hands, grinning at me the whole time in a way that can only be interpreted as insulting. She is shorter than me; blonde, blue eyes, spotless skin; slim and well-presented; but though she would be described as attractive, she radiates only negative energy.

After she dries her hands, she stops in front of the door and looks at me expectantly. I pull the door open and she steps out without a word.

When we get back Mick continues his chat with the smiling devil. I try and catch some words from my opposite end of the table, but it is hard since they are speaking so softly. The more they become engaged with one another, the more I become bored. I thought tonight was going to be interesting – playing the sub role in public; instead it is turning out to be rather tedious.

'Bitch. Keep sitting straight,' he says, turning to me.

I adjust my position appropriately but he becomes angry.

'How dare you sit on the chair like that. Move your legs to the left side of the chair, cross them properly and sit straight.'

I try and follow his instruction.

'Lift up your leg. Higher! Higher, so they will see your underwear.'

I lift my leg as high as possible. They smoke and talk together, sipping their bubbly champagne, sharing big laughs while ignoring me completely; but others find me difficult to ignore: waiters steal curious glances as they

Public Humiliation

walk by, diners gesture to one another.

Though we are a little concealed in a corner, it is still hard work to sustain this provocative posture in public.

'Hey, bitch. Keep straight and *lift – your – legs!*' he warns me again.

It's tiresome sitting there like a stick, staring at nothing. Obviously they are not brave enough to do something really bold.

'You are worthless, can't even follow my orders. What is your function in society, anyway?' he continues.

'I'm good for a beating,' I reply factually.

'You'll be beaten later, not to worry. I'm not satisfied with you at all tonight,' he says, disgusted. 'You hide away, you don't do what we tell you, you're too slow to react …'

The smiling devil says nothing but seemingly agrees as she nods her empty head. At this point I discard my submissive role and begin arguing, not satisfied with them either.

'But what am I supposed to be doing?' I ask frankly.

He pours some water on my hand – only a little and very discreetly. I smile, recalling the full glass he mentioned in one of his emails.

'That's all?' I ask, an ironic grin on my face, my expression daring him to do something bolder. Instead he looks around, nervous.

'This is so boring. You said you'd humiliate me completely in public. I thought you'd be wild, but this is nothing.'

'How can we be wild?' She has her say now. 'We can't do anything really brazen in here.'

I do not say anything, but keep looking at Mick intently. He gets furious and pulls my hair towards the table.

'You're a useless slut. You shouldn't be allowed to go out to places like this. You're nothing.'

I smile, indicating that I like the way he is talking to me right now. I can sense the attention of other guests – I do not look round, but can feel it. My eyes fill with tears, but it must be more embarrassing for them as Mick stands up from the table.

'OK, let's go. You'll get what you need.'

He throws some notes onto the table and they leave the restaurant. Following them close behind, I put on my jacket, but am immediately told off when we get outside.

'Take it off right now,' he says angrily.

In a short time he hails a cab and they sit down while I'm told to get on the floor. The party begins in earnest as they place their feet on top of me.

'Lick her shoes.'

She thrusts her high heels in front of me and I start licking, passing by with my tongue slowly and thoroughly.

'Suck her heel.'

She pushes her heel into my mouth. I suck on it,

apprehensive that she may try and break my teeth or stab my oral cavity.

'Lick my shoes again,' she says.

'All over!'

'More! More!'

While I am licking he joins in, shoving his shoes into my face. I lick their shoes one by one.

He begins kicking into me and urges her to do the same, though she does not need much encouragement. While he is busy with my arms, bottom and legs, she stabs her heels into my breasts. The pain becomes almost unbearable; I cannot keep quiet and begin moaning. *What must the driver be thinking? Surely he can hear everything?*

Mick pulls me towards him, and stares into my face with his scary big blue eyes.

'You little slut. Do you deserve all this fun?' he says, his odour of cigarettes and champagne blowing over me.

'I don't think so. You're too generous with me.' I will not let them win.

'Yes, I am indeed. It's an honour to be beaten by us.'

He throws me back to the floor. They give me some more kicks as I start to cry, my tangled hair covering my face. They're laughing at me, really enjoying humiliating me in a cab – which has the impression of being private – as we tour through central London.

Surprisingly they let up and start chatting together, resting their feet on my back as a footstool. I lift my head slightly to see the outside world, just to know where I am. Westminster Abbey goes by, Parliament, and the Home Office, our journey never seeming to end.

Suddenly he throws me into the door of the cab, and begins pushing my legs apart with both feet, asking Melanie for her assistance. He is pushing my right thigh while with her heel she stabs my left; they are spreading them so widely that I feel they may break. I start whining and crying, trying to push his shoe off with my hand. Finally, I collapse to the floor, crying wretchedly. They're giggling. When I look up, they smile, and start kicking me again. *Why is the driver not intervening? Would he not do anything even if I was beaten to death?*

Eventually, we arrive somewhere. I thought we were going to his place; instead we are outside a hotel. After we get into the lift they ask me to kneel at their feet. In the corridor I have to crawl on my knees and follow them.

'Take off your stockings, bitch,' he tells me when we enter the room. He has his belt in his hands and grins at me wickedly.

He begins whipping me all over. I'm groaning and crying.

'Keep quiet!'

'Bitch, you have to learn to be quiet. Don't make noise,' Melanie adds angrily.

'Sit on her face,' Mick instructs her.

She sits on me. She's wearing panties but I still feel

Public Humiliation

disgusted, her private parts resting on my mouth and eyes.

'I'm not a lesbian,' I mumble.

'Who said you were! Neither am I,' she says, sounding offended.

I manage to wriggle myself free from underneath her bottom, but she takes off her shoes and pokes my breasts ruthlessly. I lie on the floor sobbing with pain.

'I don't want to get cancer,' I shout at her.

'You'll not get cancer, I promise you.'

But I keep my hands in the way of her approaching high heels, so Mick decides to tie my wrists behind my back with string.

'There we go,' he says, with satisfaction.

Now there is nothing in the way of her senseless jabs. He puts his hand over my mouth as she pokes into me with pleasure ...

I'm lying there, exhausted on the floor, when she comes up to me, holding a lighted cigarette over my face.

'Open your mouth,' she says, her intention clear.

'I'm not going to be your ashtray,' I say defiantly, my hatred of them growing. 'Who on earth would let you drop ash into their body?'

'You, of course,' she says, laughing.

'Well, I'm not willing to do it.'

'You should have told us earlier. It's too late now. You have to speak up before you agree to something,' she says, with a smirk.

'You said the only limit is no sex,' Mick adds arrogantly. 'You didn't mention that we can't drop ash in your mouth.'

'You shouldn't come here saying that you can take anything when you can't,' she says with disgust.

'You are not good enough,' he states. 'You should go home, you're completely useless.'

But now I speak up, defying them, hoping to cause a rift between them:

'I think you just want to show off in front of her. You were completely satisfied when it was only us two – without her. Do you remember?'

She looks at Mick nervously before directing her venom towards me. 'What are you talking about, you fucking bitch? It's not because I'm here, you just can't do the session properly. You're not good enough – and I'm not a lesbian!'

'No, you're a self-conceited, spoilt child.'

'*What!*' she screeches. Behind the huge pile of make-up her eyes blaze with fury. 'What did you say? Who are you to tell me who I am! You fucking idiot.'

'Get out of this place right now,' Mick steps in. 'Don't ever text me again.'

'I won't. But you're the one who's texting me every day, asking "where is my little slut?" and things like that.'

Mick starts to blush as Melanie looks at him,

Public Humiliation

astonished.

'Get out of this place!' he screams.

I show him my tied hands. 'You have to take this off.'

'Go with it, I don't care.'

'But I do care, so take it off.'

He struggles with it for a while, then directs me to the bathroom and cuts it off with a razor.

'You embarrassed me in front of her,' he whispers to my ear. 'Now go, and don't ever call me again,' he says loudly.

'I'll go right after you pay me.'

'I'm not going to *pay* you!' he howls, seemingly repulsed by my suggestion.

'Yes, you will. Otherwise I'll go downstairs and talk to the receptionist, and let them know what's been going on here,' I say coolly.

'Mick, I think you should pay her,' she says.

My threat works as he takes some cash out and starts counting it.

'Fucking idiot, dumb bitch. How dare you say to me the things you said,' she continues ranting.

'OK, I won't, but I'll use any words I want to describe you in my head.'

She comes closer and closer to me, looking as though she will explode.

'So say it again, you fucking bitch. What do you think of me?' She slaps my cheek.

'Hey darling, the game is over,' I warn her, with an amazingly wide smile that drives her crazy.

'Why are you smiling like that? Ha, you think it's funny. Fucking bitch!'

She pushes me against the wall. I feel like saying some very nasty things to her right now, but my ironic smile seems to be more than sufficient.

'Just calm down, darling,' I say, trying to look relaxed.

She goes over to the bed and starts jumping on it hysterically. 'Why are you smiling? You're a FREAK! WHERE THE FUCKING FREAK DO YOU COME FROM?'

Her face becomes a ball of angry wrinkles which starts to worry me – she looks simply furious. He steps in with the intention of banging my head against the door but I raise my voice to remind him that it is over. Finally he hands me the cash.

They both look incensed as I walk out the door, triumphant.

15

New Beginnings?

The next morning I wake in terrible pain. There are yellow and blue marks covering my breasts, and it hurts every time I take a breath, even a small one. I'm upset, and I want him to know it.

> /I can hardly breathe and move right now. Feeling great pain in my breasts that were kicked by that arrogant bitch. I might need to have an x-ray they hurt so much./

He texts back.

> /If complications arise - and it may be that

On Undefended Flesh

you are just sore at this point - please let me know - seriously - and I will take care of it. In no way was anything supposed to be terribly hurtful./

/And you did not pay me the promised amount./

/You are correct - I will pay you the rest of the money - it was wrong not to. Now I like you as my slut - and want to continue - more of the cab - a redo of the restaurant humiliation - this time in the 'right' venue. If we do continue - she will not be there - since I don't think you like it with her./

/Did she say anything about me afterwards?/

/Yes - she said she wants to really beat you next time. Can you take it? Maybe you two can go at each other. But be careful - if she does get the better of you - there will be a lot more hurting than your tits. You will probably end up on the short end - want to try?/

/She is an aggressive and violent woman. She was very cruel and so are you./

New Beginnings?

/That is her nature. Told you she had a slave once - you should have seen her after she got done with her - week after week. I had compassion for you - but I thought you could take it — and it was a pleasure for me to watch./

/Just a couple more questions. Do you think the cab driver saw anything? Why did Melanie go so crazy?/

/Yes - the cab driver saw ALL. He looked in his mirror several times and listened intently. Saw you sucking Melanie's heels - remember how she pushed your head against the cab wall and you took the whole heel down your throat - almost made me cum. Did look at me when we got out - he smiled.
She got so mad because you actually could control her - no matter what she did to you./

The whole day I stay home recuperating. Pete sends me some new texts:

/I'm back from holiday in USA. Still would like to arrange session with you. Am in London a lot the next few weeks. Text me if possible./

On Undefended Flesh

/Please send just one text saying you are OK for £400 session in Bayswater in 2 weeks. Just fair spanking, nothing brutal. Can we meet up again, please? I do rate you highly as a spankee girl – you know that./

Yes, I know that Pete, but I don't feel like being beaten by you, or anyone else for that matter. After that whole cruel tit-torture, I think it is time to stop. Though I have learned a lot about myself and other people, and in the process discovered a world that I would never have believed existed, I'm fed up with being a miserable submissive. I need to turn over a new leaf. Actually, I need to sort out my life and do something with it.

*

A few weeks later as I'm going through my emails, I notice an intriguing response to my old *Good Girl Loves Being Used and Abused and Exploited* ad:

If that is what you really desire then you need not look further. However, let it be known: I am an extremely sadistic and brutal pervert.

I wish to give you a DRASTIC beating with a thick leather strap (only because it leaves less of a mark). Nevertheless, it will hurt A LOT. Therefore you will have to be restrained to a wooden frame. Due to the intense pain you will be screaming and begging me

New Beginnings?

to stop. But I stop for no one, especially when I am enjoying myself.

The venue will be a warehouse where the walls are extremely thick. Should you faint, cold water will be used to bring you around. I propose two hours of beatings — not continual, but with breaks so that you have time to recover. This will prove to be a significant experience in your — up to now — pathetic little life.

Of course, financial compensation will be in line with the ordeal that you will be put through. You will be required to sign a consent agreement. It will be done in a European country where the laws allow this kind of consenting behaviour. You will be flown by private aircraft both ways. Due to the nature of this activity, personal injury cannot be ruled out. Should any occur, I will have you sent to a private hospital for treatment.

I have done this many times before. Of the women involved, some have been mentally traumatised. This may be the experience that you have always desired. Up to now you have probably come across pathetic men. This will be the REAL THING! The ULTIMATE experience. So only reply after you have given your deep and full consideration.

_____@

It does make me think ...